March of America Facsimile Series

Number 12

Virginia Richly Valued

Richard Hakluyt

Virginia
Richly Valued

by Richard Hakluyt

ANN ARBOR

UNIVERSITY MICROFILMS, INC.

A Subsidiary of Xerox Corporation

Foreword

Virginia Richly Valued, by the Description of the Main Land of Florida, Her Next Neighbor, printed in London in 1609, is the first description in English of the continental interior of the Southern and Gulf states and of the discovery of the Mississippi River.

"Florida" to the Spanish conquistadores of the early sixteenth century meant all of North America, the extent of which was still unguessed. To Hernando (or Fernando) de Soto and his famous expedition of 1538-1543 it came to mean the weary trek from Tampa Bay through what is now Florida, Georgia, the Carolinas, Tennessee, Alabama, and Mississippi to the great river which was journey's end for de Soto. Falling "into great dumps to see how hard it was to get to the sea, and worse, because his men and horses every day diminished," the hitherto indomitable leader took to his bed and shortly, "being evil handled with fevers," died. In the Mississippi's opaque and anonymous waters his men buried him, to conceal from the Indians the fact that Christians, contrary to de Soto's claim, were not immortal. The survivors pushed on for the better part of a year, across the Red River into Texas, before abandoning the search for such treasure as the Incas had. They backtracked to the Mississippi and followed it south to the sea, 311 of the original company of 600 arriving "again into Christendom" at Veracruz, Mexico, in the autumn of 1543.

The original account of the expedition, entitled *Relaçam verdadeira dos trabalhos*, was written by a Portuguese "gentleman of Elvas" (a town in Portugal) who was a member of the company. Presumably he was one of the eight volunteers from Elvas listed on page 5, most probably the last named, Alvaro Fernandez. The narrative gives evidence of having been written from memory after the author's return home. It was published at Evora, Portugal, in 1557.

The half-century between the Portuguese and English publications represents almost precisely the period in which England caught up with Portugal and Spain on the high seas. Richard Hakluyt, great collector and editor of *The Principal Navigations, Voyages and Discoveries of the English Nation* (1589-1590 and 1598-1600), had long been a propagandist for English colonization. He was a member of the Virginia Company of London that founded Jamestown in 1607 and that issued stock for public purchase in 1609, publication year of *Virginia Richly Valued*. With his translated account of the "riches and fertility" of neighboring Florida, Hakluyt hoped to enlist recruits for the struggling Virginia colony. After Jamestown's "Starving Time" of the winter of 1609-1610, another issue was brought out with the less provocative title of *The Worthy and Famous History of the Travels, Discovery, and Conquest of Terra Florida* (1611).

A modern translation by Buckingham Smith from the Portuguese original is to be found in *Spanish Explorers in the Southern United States, 1528-1543*, edited by Theodore H. Lewis, Original Narrative Series (New York, [1953]).

Virginia Richly Valued

VIRGINIA
richly valued,

By the description of the maine land of Florida, her next neighbour:

Out of the foure yeeres continuall trauell and discouerie, for aboue one thousand miles East and West, of *Don Ferdinando de Soto*, and sixe hundred able men in his companie.

Wherin are truly obserued the riches and fertilitie of those parts, abounding with things necessarie, pleasant, and profitable for the life of man: with the natures and dispositions of the Inhabitants.

Written by a Portugall gentleman of *Eluas*, emploied in all the action; and translated out of Portugese by Richard Hakluyt.

AT LONDON

Printed by Felix Kyngston for *Matthew Lownes*, and are to be sold at the signe of the Bishops head in Pauls Churchyard.
1609.

TO THE RIGHT
HONOVRABLE, THE
Right Worſhipfull Counſellors, and
others the cheerefull aduenturors for
the aduancement of that Chriſtian
and noble plantation in
VIRGINIA.

*His worke, right Honourable, right Wor-
ſhipfull, and the reſt, though ſmall in
ſhew, yet great in ſubſtance, doth yeeld
much light to our enterpriſe now on foot:
whether you deſire to know the preſent
and future commodities of our countrie;
or the qualities and conditions of the Inhabitants, or what
courſe is beſt to be taken with them.*

Touching the commodities, beſides the generall report of
Cabeça de Vaca *to* Charles *the Emperour (who firſt trauelled through a great part of the Inland of* Florida, *next
adioyning vpon our* Virginia) *That* Florida *was the richeſt countrie of the world; and, that after hee had
found clothes made of cotton wooll, he ſaw gold and* Chap 35.
ſiluer, and ſtones of great value: I referre you firſt to the
rich mines of gold reported to be in the prouince of* Yupaha,
*and deſcribed in the twelfth Chapter of this Treatiſe to come
within our limits: And againe, to the copper hatchets found
in* Cutifachiqui, *ſtanding vpon the Riuer of* Santa Hele-

A 2   na,

The Epiſtle Dedicatorie.

na, *which were ſaid to haue a mixture of gold. It ſeemeth alſo that the laſt Chronicler of the Weſt Indies*, Antonio de Herrera, *ſpeaking of the foreſaid Riuer of* Santa Helena, *which ſtandeth in* 32. *degrees and an halfe, alludeth to the* Decad.3.lib.8. cap.8. *prouince of* Yupaha, *in theſe words :* Y el oro, y plata, que hallaron, no era de aquella tierra, ſino de 60. leguas, adentro al norte, de los pueblos dichos Otapales y Olagatanos, adonde ſe intiende, que ay minas de oro, plata, y cobre. *That is to ſay, That the gold and ſiluer which they found, was not of that countrie (of* Santa Helena) *but* 60. *leagues diſtant toward the North, of the townes called* Otapales *and* Olagatanos, *where we vnderſtand that there are mines of gold, ſiluer, and copper. By which reckoning theſe rich mines are in the latitude of* 35. *degrees and an halfe. I deſire you likewiſe to take knowledge of the famous golden prouince of* Chiſca, *ſtretching further to the North, where-* Chap.15. *of the Cacique of* Coſte *gaue notice to* Ferdinando de Soto *in the towne of* Chiaha, *affirming, that there were mines of copper, and of another mettall of the ſame colour, ſaue that it was finer, and of a farre more perfect luſtre, and farre better in ſight, and that they vſed it not ſo much, becauſe it was ſofter. And the ſelfeſame thing was before told the Gouernour in* Cutifachiqui : *who ſent two Chriſtians from* Chiaha *with certaine Indians which knew the countrie of* Chiſca, *and the language thereof, to view it, and to make report of* Chap.23. *that which they ſhould finde. We likewiſe reade not long af-ter, that the Gouernour ſet forward to ſeeke a prouince called* Pacaha, *which hee was informed to be neere vnto* Chiſca, *where the Indians told him, that there was gold. And in* Chap.24. *another place hee ſaith ;* That *from* Pacaha *hee ſent thirtie horſemen and fiftie footmen to the prouince of* Caluça, *to ſee if from thence he might trauell to* Chiſca, *where the Indians ſaid, there was a worke of gold and copper. So that here is*

foure

The Epistle Dedicatorie.

foure times mention, and that in sundrie places, of the rich
and famous golde mines of Chisca, and that they lie beyond
the mountaines toward the North, ouer which they were not
able to trauell for the roughnes thereof. But what neede I to
stand vpon forren testimonies, since Master Thomas He-
riot, a man of much iudgement in these causes, signified vnto you all, at your late solemne meeting at the house of the right
honourable the Earle of Exeter; how to the Southwest of our
old fort in Virginia, the Indians often informed him, that
there was a great melting of red mettall, reporting the manner in working of the same. Besides, our owne Indians haue
lately reuealed either this or another rich mine of copper or
gold in a towne called Ritanoe, neere certaine mountaines
lying West of Roanoac.

Another very gainfull commoditie is, the huge quantitie
of excellent perles, and little babies and birds made of them,
that were found in Cutifachiqui. The abundance whereof
is reported to be such, that if they would haue searched diuers Chap. 14.
graues in townes thereabout, they might haue laded many of
their horses. Neither are the Turkie stones and cotton wooll
found at Guasco to be forgotten, nor passed ouer in silence.

But that, which I make no small account of, is, the multitude of Oxen, which, from the beginning of the 16. to the
end of the 26. Chapter, are nine seuerall times made mention
of, and that along from Chiaha, Coste, Pacaha, Coligoa,
and Tulla, still toward the North, to wit, toward vs, there
was such store of them, that they could keepe no corne for
them: and that the Indians liued vpon their flesh. The haire
of these Oxen is likewise said to be like a soft wooll, betweene
the course and fine wooll of sheepe: and that they vse them
for couerlets, because they are very soft and woolled like sheep:
and not so onely, but they make bootes, shooes, targets, and
other things necessarie of the same. Besides the former bene-

A 3   fits,

fits; their young ones may be framed to the yoke, for carting and tillage of our ground. And I am in good hope, that ere it be long we shall haue notice of their being neerer vs, by that which I reade in the Italian relation of Cabeça de Vaca, the first finder of them, which writeth, That they spread themselues within the countrie aboue foure hundred leagues. Moreouer, Vasques de Coronado, and long after him, Antonio de Espejo (whose voiages are at large in my third volume) trauelled many leagues among these heards of Oxen, and found them from 33. degrees ranging very farre to the North and Northeast.

A fourth chiefe commoditie wee may account to be the great number of Mulberrie trees, apt to feede Silke-wormes to make silke : whereof there was such plentie in many places, that, though they found some hempe in the countrie, the Spaniards made ropes of the barks of them for their brigandines, when they were to put to sea for Noua Hispania.

A fifth is the excellent and perfect colours, as black, white, greene, yellow, and red, and the materials to dye withall, so often spoken of in this discourse : among which I haue some hope to bring you to the knowledge of the rich graine of Cochanillio, so much esteemed, and of so great price. I speake nothing of the seuerall sorts of passing good grapes for Wine and Raisons.

Chap. 31. & 32 Neither is it the least benefit, that they found salt made by the Indians at Cayas, and in two places of the prouince of Aguacay : the manner also how the Inhabitants make it, is very well worth the obseruation.

One of the chiefest of all the rest may be the notice of the Chap. 31. & 32 South Sea, leading vs to Iapan and China, which I finde here twice to be spoken of. Whereof long since I haue written a discourse, which I thinke not fit to be made ouer common.

For closing vp this point, The distances of places, the qualities

The Epistle Dedicatorie.

lities of the soiles, the situations of the regions, the diuersities and goodnesse of the fruits, the seuerall sorts of beasts, the varietie of fowles, the difference betweene the Inhabitants of the mountaines and the plaines, and the riches of the Inland in comparison of the Seacoast, are iudicially set downe in the conclusion of this booke, whereunto for mine owne ease I referre you.

To come to the second generall head, which in the beginning I proposed, concerning the manners and dispositions of the Inhabitants: among other things, I finde them here noted to be very eloquent and well spoken, as the short Orations, interpreted by Iohn Ortiz, which liued twelue yeeres among them, make sufficient proofe. And the author, which was a gentleman of Eluas in Portugall, emploied in all the action, whose name is not set downe, speaking of the Cacique of Tulla, saith, that aswell this Cacique, as the others, and all those which came to the Gouernour on their behalfe, deliuered their message or speech in so good order, that no Oratour could vtter the same more eloquently. But for all their faire and cunning speeches, they are not ouermuch to be trusted: for they be the greatest traitors of the world, as their manifold most craftie contriued and bloody treasons, here set down at large, doe euidently proue. They be also as vnconstant as the wethercock, and most readie to take all occasions of aduantages to doe mischiefe. They are great liars and dissemblers; for which faults often times they had their deserued paiments. And many times they gaue good testimonie of their great valour and resolution. To handle them gently, while gentle courses may be found to serue, it will be without comparison the best: but if gentle polishing will not serue, then we shall not want hammerours and rough masons enow, I meane our old soldiours trained vp in the Netherlands, to square and prepare them to our Preachers hands. To conclude,

The Epistle Dedicatorie.

clude, I trust by your Honours and Worships wise instructions to the noble Gouernour, the worthy experimented Lieutenant and Admirall, and other chiefe managers of the businesse, all things shall be so prudently carried, that the painfull Preachers shall be reuerenced and cherished, the valiant and forward soldiour respected, the diligent rewarded, the coward emboldened, the weake and sick relieued, the mutinous suppressed, the reputation of the Christians among the Saluages preserued, our most holy faith exalted, all Paganisme and Idolatrie by little and little vtterly extinguished. And here reposing and resting my selfe vpon this sweete hope, I cease, beseeching the Almightie to blesse this good work in your hands to the honour and glorie of his most holy name, to the inlargement of the dominions of his sacred Maiestie, and to the generall good of all the worthie Aduenturers and vndertakers. From my lodging in the Colledge of Westminster this 15. of Aprill, 1609.

> By one publikely and anciently deuoted to Gods seruice, and all yours in this so good action,

Richard Hakluyt.

A RELATION
OF SVCH THINGS, AS

Don Ferdinando De Soto,
the Adelantado of *Florida* paſſed in ſeeking to conquer the ſaid Countrey : wherein is declared who he was,
and what ſome of them were that went with him: and
ſome particulars and diuerſities of the Countrie,
and whatſoeuer they ſaw and happened
vnto them in the ſame.

CHAP. I.

Which declareth who Don Ferdinando de Soto *was,
and how he got the gouernment of* Florida.

Aptaine *Soto* was the ſon of a Squire
of *Xerez* of *Badaioz*. He went into the
Spaniſh *Indies*, when *Peter Arias* of
Auila was Gouernour of the Weſt
Indies : And there he was without
any thing elſe of his owne, ſaue his
ſword and target : and for his good qualities and
valour, *Peter Arias* made him Captaine of a troope of
horſemen, and by his commandement hee went
with *Fernando Pizarro* to the conqueſt of *Peru* : where
(as many perſons of credit reported, which were
there preſent) as well at the taking of *Atabalipa*, Lord
of *Peru*, as at the aſſault of the citie of *Cuſco*, and in

B   all

all other places where they found resistance, wheresoeuer hee was present, hee passed all other Captaines
and principall persons. For which cause, besides his
part of the treasure of *Atabalipa*, he had a good share:
whereby in time he gathered an hundred and fourescore thousand Duckets together, with that which fell
to his part: which he brought into *Spaine*: whereof the
Emperour borrowed a certaine part, which he repaied
againe with 60000 Rials of plate in the rent of the
silkes of *Granada*, and all the rest was deliuered him in
the Contractation house of *Siuil*. He tooke seruants, to
wit, a Steward, a Gentleman Vsher, Pages, a Gentleman of the Horse, a Chamberlaine, Lackies, and al other
officers that the house of a Noble mã requireth. From
Siuil hee went to the Court, and in the Court, there
accompanied him *Iohn Danusco* of *Siuil*, and *Lewis
Moscoso D'aluarado*, *Nunno de Touar*, and *Iohn Rodriguez Lobillo*. Except *Iohn Danusco*, all the rest came
with him from *Peru*: and euery one of them brought
fourteene or fifteene thousand Duckets: all of them
went well and costly apparrelled. And although *Soto*
of his owne nature was not liberall, yet because that
was the first time that hee was to shew himselfe in the
Court, he spent frankely, and went accompanied with
those which I haue named, and with his seruants, and
many other which resorted vnto him. Hee married
with *Donna Isabella de Bouadilla*, daughter of *Peter Arias* of *Auila*, Earle of *Punno en Rostro*. The Emperour
made him the Gouernor of the Isle of *Cuba*, and Adelantado or President of *Florida*; with a title of Marques of certaine part of the lands, that he should conquer.

Chap. II.

How Cabeça de Vaca *came to the Court, and gaue relation of the Countrie of* Florida : *And of the Companie that was assembled in* Siuil *to goe with* Don Ferdinando de Soto.

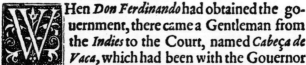

WHen *Don Ferdinando* had obtained the gouernment, there came a Gentleman from the *Indies* to the Court, named *Cabeça de Vaca,* which had been with the Gouernor *Pamphilo de Naruaez* which died in *Florida,* who reported that *Naruaez* was cast away at sea with all the companie ẏ went with him. And how he with foure more escaped and arriued in *Nueua Espanna:* Also he brought a relation in writing of that which hee had seene in *Florida* ; which said in some places : In such a place I haue seene this ; and the rest which here I saw, I leaue to conferre of betweene his Maiestie and my selfe. Generally he reported the miserie of the Countrie, and the troubles which hee passed : and hee told some of his kinsfolke, which were desirous to goe into the *Indies,* and vrged him very much to tell them whether he had seene any rich country in *Florida,* that he might not tell them, because hee and another, whose name was *Orantes,* (who remained in *Nueua Espanna* with purpose to returne into *Florida :* for which intent hee came into *Spaine* to beg the gouernment thereof of the Emperour) had sworne not to discouer some of those things which they had seene, because no man should preuent them in begging the same : And hee informed them, *That it was the richest Countrie of the world. Don Ferdinando de Soto* was very desirous to haue

Florida is the richest Cortrie of the world.

B 2

haue him with him, and made him a fauourable offer :
and after they were agreed, becaufe *Soto* gaue him not
a fumme of money which he demanded to buy a fhip,
they broke off againe. *Baltafar de Gallegos*, and *Chriſto-*
pher de Spindola, the kinfemen of *Cabeça de Vaca*, told
him, that for that which hee had imparted to them,
they were refolued to paſſe with *Soto* into *Florida*, and
therefore they prayed him to aduife them what they
were beſt to doe. *Cabeça de Vaca* told them, that the
cauſe why he went not with *Soto* was, becaufe hee hoped to beg another gouernment, and that hee was loth
to goe vnder the command of another : and that hee
came to beg the conqueſt of *Florida :* but feeing *Don*
Ferdinando de Soto had gotten it alreadie, for his othes
fake hee might tell them nothing of that which they
would know : but hee counfelled them to fell their
goods and goe with him, and that in fo doing they
fhould doe well. Aſſoone as he had opportunitie hee
fpake with the Emperour, and related vnto him whatfoeuer hee had paſſed and feene, and come to vnderſtand. Of this relation made by word of mouth to the
Emperour, the Marques of *Aſtorga* had notice, and
forthwith determined to fend with *Don Ferdinando*
de Soto his brother *Don Antonio Oſorio :* & with him two
kinfmen of his prepared themfelues, to wit, *Francis O-*
forio, and *Garcia Oſorio*. *Don Antonio* difpoſſeſſed himfelfe of 60000 Rials of rent which hee held by the
Church: and *Francis Oſorio* of a town of Vaſſals, which
he had in the Countrie *de Campos*. And they made
their Rendezuous with the Adelantado in *Siuil*. The
like did *Nunnez de Touar*, and *Lewis de Moſcofo*, and
Iohn Rodriguez Lobillo, each of whō had brought from
Peru fourteene or fifteene thoufand Duckets. *Lewis de*
Moſcofo

Moscoso carried with him two brethren: there went also *Don Carlos*, which had married the Gouernours Neece, and tooke her with him. From *Badaioz* there went *Peter Calderan*, and three kinsemen of the Adelantado, to wit, *Arias Tinoco, Alfonso Romo*, and *Diego Tinoco*. And as *Lewis de Moscoso* passed through * *Eluas, Andrew de Vasconcelos* spake with him, and requested him to speake to *Don Ferdinando de Soto* concerning him, and deliuered him certaine warrants which he had receiued from the Marques of *Villa real*, wherein he gaue him the Captaineship of *Ceuta* in *Barbarie*, that he might shew them vnto him. And the Adelantado saw them; and was informed who hee was, and wrote vnto him, that hee would fauour him in all things, and by al meanes, and would giue him a charge of men in *Florida*. And from *Eluas* went *Andrew de Vasconcelos*, and *Fernan Pegado, Antonio Martinez Segurado, Men Roiz Pereira, Iohn Cordero, Stephen Pegado, Benedict Fernandez*, and *Aluaro Fernandez*. And out of *Salamanca*, and *Iaen*, and *Valencia*, and *Albuquerque*, and from other partes of *Spaine*, many people of Noble birth assembled at *Siuil:* insomuch that in Saint *Lucar* many men of good account which had sold their goods remained behind for want of shipping, wheras for other known and rich Countries, they are wont to want men: and this fell out by occasion of that which *Cabeça de Vaca* told the Emperour, and informed such persons as hee had conference withall touching the State of that Countrie. *Soto* made him great offers: and being agreed to goe with him (as I haue said before) because he would not giue him monie to pay for a ship, which he had bought, they brake off, & he went for Gouernour to the Riuer of *Plate*. His kinsemen

Christopher

Eluas is a Citie in Portugal.

Cabeça de Vaca was the Gouernour of the Riuer of Plate.

*Chriſtoper de Spindola,*and *Baltaſar de Gallegos* went with
S**o**. *Baltaſar de Gallegos* ſold houſes and vineyards,and
rent corne,and ninetie rankes of Oliue trees in the *Xa-
raſe* of *Siuil :* Hee had the office of *Alcalde Mayor,* and
tooke his wife with him : And there went alſo many
other perſons of account with the Preſident, and had
the offices following by great friendſhip,becauſe they
were offices deſired of many : to wit,*Antonie de Biedma*
was Factor,*Iohn Danuſco* was Auditor,and *Iohn Gaytan*
nephew to the Cardinall of *Ciguenȝa* had the office of
Treaſurer.

Chap. III.

How the Portugales went to Siuil, *and from thence to*
S. Lucar : *he appointed Captaines ouer the ſhips, and
diſtributed the people which were to goe in them.*

He Portugales departed from *Eluas* the 15.
of Ianuarie, and came to *Siuil* the 19.of
the ſame moneth,and went to the lodging
of the Gouernor,and entred into a court,
ouer the which were certaine galleries where hee was,
who came downe and receiued them at the ſtaires,
whereby they went vp into the galleries : when he was
come vp,he commanded chaires to be giuen them to
ſit on. And *Andrew de Vaſconcelos* told him who hee
and the other Portugales were, and how they all were
come to accompany him, and ſerue him in his voiage.
He gaue him thanks,and made ſhew of great contentment for his comming and offer. And the table being
alreadie laid he inuited them to dinner. And being at
dinner he commanded his ſteward to ſeeke a lodging
for them neere vnto his owne,where they might bee
lodged.

lodged. The Adelantado departed from *Siuil* to Saint
Lucar with al the people which were to goe with him:
And he commanded a muster to be made, at the which
the Portugales shewed themselues armed in verie
bright armour, and the Castellans very gallant with
silke vpon silke, with many pinkings and cuts. The Gouernour, because these brauaries in such an action did
not like him, commanded that they should muster a-
nother day, and euery one should come foorth with
his armour: at the which the Portugales came as at the
first armed with very good armour. The Gouernour
placed them in order neere vnto the standard which
the ensigne-bearer carried. The Castellanes for the
most part did weare very bad and rustie shirts of maile,
and all of them headpeeces and steele cappes, and very
bad lances. And some of them sought to come among
the Portugales. So those passed and were counted and
enroled, which *Soto* liked and accepted of, and did accompanie him into *Florida* ; which were in all sixe
hundred men. He had alreadie bought seuen ships,
and had all necessarie prouision aboord them : He appointed Captaines, and deliuered to euery one his
ship, and gaue them in a role what people euery one
should carrie with them.

Sixe hundred
men went
with Soto in-
to Florida.

C H A P.

CHAP. IV.

How the Adelantado with his people departed from Spaine, and came to the Canaries, and afterward to the Antiles.

IN the yeere of our Lord 1538. in the moneth of Aprill, the Adelantado deliuered his shippes to the Captaines which were to goe in them : and tooke for himselfe a new ship, and good of saile, and gaue another to *Andrew de Vasconcelos*, in which the Portugales went : hee went ouer the barre of S.*Lucar* on Sunday being S.*Lazarus* day, in the morning, of the moneth and yeere aforesaid, with great ioy, commanding his trumpets to be sounded, and many shots of the ordinance to be discharged. Hee sailed foure daies with a prosperous wind ; and suddenly it calmed : the calmes continued eight daies with swelling seas, in such wise, that wee made no way. The 15. day after his departure from S. *Lucar*, hee came to *Gomera*, one of the *Canaries*, on Easter day in the morning. The Earle of that Island was apparrelled all in white, cloke, ierkin, hose, shooes, and cappe, so that hee seemed a Lord of the Gypses. He receiued the Gouernour with much ioy : hee was well lodged, and all the rest had their lodgings gratis, and gat great store of victuals for their monie, as bread, wine and flesh : and they tooke what was needfull for their ships : and the Sunday following, eight daies after their arriuall, they departed from the Isle of *Gomera*. The Earle gaue to *Donna Isabella* the Adelantados wife a bastard daughter that hee had to bee her waiting maid. They arriued at the *Antilles*, in the Isle of

of *Cuba*, at the port of the City of *Sant Iago* vpon Whit-
funday. Affone as they came thither, a Gentleman
of the Citie fent to the fea fide a very faire roan horfe
and well furnifhed for the Gouernour, and a mule for
Donna Ifabella : and all the horfemen and footemen
that were in the towne came to receiue him at the fea-
fide. The Gouernour was well lodged, vifited, and
ferued of all the inhabitants of that Citie, and all his
companie had their lodgings freely : thofe which defired to goe into the countrie, were diuided by foure
and foure, and fixe and fixe in the farmes or granges,
according to the abilitie of the owners of the farmes,
and were furnifhed by them with all things neceffary.

Chap. V.

*Of the inhabitants which are in the Citie of S. Iago, and
in the other townes of the Iſland : and of the qualitie of
the foile, and fruites that it yeeldeth.*

He Citie of S. *Iago* hath fourefcore houfes which are great and well contriued.
The moft part haue their walles made of
bords, & are couered with thatch; it hath
fome houfes builded with lime & ftone,
and couered with tiles. It hath great Orchards and
many trees in them, differing from thofe of *Spaine :*
there be figgetrees which beare figges as big as ones **Great figges.**
fift, yellow within, and of fmall tafte ; and other trees
which beare a fruit which they call Ananes, in making **Ananes.**
and bignes like to a fmall Pineapple : it is a fruit very
fweete in tafte : the fhel being taken away, the kernel is
like a peece of frefh cheefe. In the granges abroad in **Great Pine-**
the countrie there are other great pineapples, which **apples.**

C grow

Erua babofa.

grow on low trees, and are like the * Aloetree: they are of a very good fmell and exceeding good tafte. Other trees do beare a fruit, which they call Mameis of the bignes of Peaches. This the Iflanders do hold for the beft fruit of the country. There is another fruit which they call Guayabas like Filberds, as bigge as figges. There are other trees as high as a iaueline, hauing one only ftocke without any bough, and the leaues as long as a cafting dart: and the fruite is of the bigneffe and fafhion of a Cucumber, one bunch beareth 20. or 30. and as they ripen, the tree bendeth downeward with them: they are called in this countrie Plantanos; and are of a good tafte, & ripen after they be gathered; but thofe are the better which ripen vpon the tree it felfe; they beare fruite but once: and the tree being cut downe, there fpring vp others out of the but, which beare fruite the next yeere. There is another fruit; whereby many people are fuftained, and chiefly the flaues, which are called Batatas. Thefe grow now in the Ifle of *Terçera*, belonging to the Kingdome of *Portugal*, and they grow within the earth, and are like a fruit called Iname, they haue almoft ÿ tafte of a cheftnut. The bread of this countrie is alfo made of rootes which are like the Batatas. And the ftocke whereon thofe rootes doe grow is like an Elder tree: they make their ground in little hillocks, and in each of them they thruft 4. or 5. ftakes; and they gather the rootes a yeere and an halfe after they fet them. If any one, thinking it is a Batata or Potato roote, chance to eate of it neuer fo little, hee is in great danger of death: which was feene by experience in a fouldier, which affone as hee had eaten a very little of one of thofe rootes, hee died quicklie. They pare thefe rootes and ftampe them, and

Mameis, an excellent fruit.

Guayabas.

Plantanos.

Batatas, or Potatos.

The Caffaui roote.

squefe

squese them in a thing like a presse: the iuyce that commeth from them is of an euill smell. The bread is of little taste and lesse substance. Of the fruites of *Spaine*, there are Figges and Oranges, and they beare fruit all the yeere, because the soile is very ranke and fruitfull. In this countrie are many good horses, and there is greene grasse all the yeere. There be many wild oxen and hogges, whereby the people of the Island is well furnished with flesh: Without the townes abroad in the Countrie are many fruites. And it happeneth sometimes that a Christian goeth out of the way and is lost 15. or 20. daies, because of the many paths in the thicke groues that crosse to and fro made by the oxen: and being thus lost, they sustaine themselues with fruites and palmîtos: for there bee many great groues of Palme trees through all the Island: they yeeld no other fruite that is of any profit. The Isle of *Cuba* is 300. leagues long from the East to the West, and is in some places 30. in others 40. leagues from North to South. It hath 6. townes of Christians: to wit, S. *Iago*, *Baracôa*, *Bayamo*, *Puerto de Principes*, S. *Espirito*, and *Hauana*. Euery one hath betweene 30. and 40. households, except S. *Iago* and *Hauana*, which haue about 60. or 80. houses. They haue Churches in each of them, and a Chaplen which confesseth them and saith Masse. In S. *Iago* is a Monasterie of Franciscan Friers: it hath but few Friers, and is well prouided of almes, because the countrie is rich: The Church of S. *Iago* hath honest reuenew, and there is a Curat and Prebends and many Priests, as the Church of that Citie, which is the chiefe of all the Island. There is in this countrie much gold, and few slaues to get it: For

Store of good horses.

The length and breadth of Cuba.

many

many haue made away themfelues, becaufe of the
Chriftians euill vfage of them in the mines. A ftew-
A wittie ftra- ard of *Vafques Porcallo,* which was an inhabitour in that
tagem. Ifland, vnderftanding that his flaues would make away
themfelues, ftaied for them with a cudgill in his hand
at the place where they were to meete, and told them,
that they could neither doe nor thinke any thing,
that hee did not know before ; and that hee came
thither to kill himfelfe with them, to the end, that
if hee had vfed them badly in this world, hee might
vfe them worfe in the world to come : And this was
a meane that they changed their purpofe, and turned home againe to doe that which he commanded
them.

Chap. VI.

How the Gouernour fent Donna Ifabella *with the ſhips
to* Hauana, *and he with ſome of his people went thither by land.*

He Gouernour fent from S. *Iago* his
Nephew *Don Carlos* with the ſhips
in company of *Donna Ifabella* to tarrie for him at *Hauana,* which is an
hauen in the Weft part toward the
head of the Ifland, 180. leagues
from the Citie of Saint *Iago.* The
Gouernour and thofe which ftaied with him bought
horfes and proceeded on their iournie. The firft
Bayamo. towne they came vnto was *Bayamo :* they were lodged foure and foure, and fixe and fixe, as they went in
company, and where they lodged, they tooke nothing
for their diet, for nothing coft them ought faue the
Maiz

Maiz or corne for their horſes, becauſe the Gouernor went to viſit them from towne to towne, and ſeaſed them in the tribute and ſeruice of the Indians. *Bayamo* is 25. leagues from the Citie of S. *Iago*. Neere vnto the towne paſſeth a great Riuer, which is called *Tanto*; it is greater then *Guadiana*, and in it be very great Crocodiles, which ſometimes hurt the Indians, or the cattell which paſſeth the Riuer. In all the countrie are neither Wolfe, Foxe, Beare, Lion, nor Tiger. There are wild dogges which goe from the houſes into the woods and feed vpon ſwine. There be certaine Snakes as bigge as a mans thigh or bigger, they are very ſlow, they doe no kind of hurt. From *Bayamo* to *Puerto dellos principes* are 50. leagues. In al the Iſland from towne to towne, the way is made by ſtubbing vp the vnderwood : and if it bee left but one yeere vndone, the wood groweth ſo much, that the way cannot be ſeene, and the paths of the oxen are ſo many, that none can trauell without an Indian of the Countrie for a guide: for all the reſt is very hie and thicke woods. From *Puerto dellos principes* the Gouernour went to the houſe of *Vaſques Porcallo* by ſea in a bote, (for it was neere the ſea) to know there ſome newes of *Donna Iſabella*, which at that inſtant (as afterward was knowne) was in great diſtreſſe, in ſo much that the ſhips loſt one another : and two of them fell on the coaſt of *Florida*, and all of them endured great want of water and victuals. When the ſtorme was ouer, they met together, without knowing where they were : in the end they deſcried the Cape of S. *Anton*, a countrie not inhabited of the Iſland of *Cuba* : there they watered ; and at the end of 40. daies, which were paſſed ſince their departure from the City of S. *Iago*, they ariued at *Hauana*.

Puerto dellos Principes.

The Cape of S. Antonio.

C 3   The

The Gouernour was presently informed thereof, and went to *Donna Isabella.* And those which went by land, which were one hundred and fiftie horsemen, being diuided into two parts, because they would not oppresse the inhabitants, trauelled by S. *Espirito,* which is 60. leagues from *Puerto dellos principes.* The food which they carried with them was *Caçabe* bread, which is that whereof I made mention before: and it is of such a qualitie, that if it be wet, it breaketh presently, whereby it happened to some to eate flesh without bread for many daies. They carried dogges with them, and a man of the Country, which did hunt; & by the way, or where they were to lodge that night, they killed as many hogges as they needed. In this iournie they were well prouided of beefe and porke: And they were greatly troubled with Muskitos, especially in a lake, which is called the mere of *Pia,* which they had much adoe to passe from noone till night, the water might be some halfe league ouer, and to be swome about a crossebow shot, the rest came to the waste, and they waded vp to the knees in the mire, and in the bottome were cockle shels, which cut their feete very sore; in such sort, that there was neither boote nor shooe sole that was hole at halfe way. Their clothes and saddels were passed in baskets of Palme trees. Passing this lake, stripped out of their clothes, there came many muskitos, vpon whose biting there arose a wheale that smarted very much: they strooke them with their hands, and with the blowe which they gaue they killed so many, that the blood did runne downe the armes and bodies of the men. That night they rested very little for them, and other nights also in the like places and times. They came to *Santo Espirito,* which is a towne

Santo Espirito.

of

of thirtie houses; there passeth by it a little Riuer: it is very pleasant and fruitfull, hauing great store of Oranges and citrons, and fruites of the Countrie: One halfe of the companie were lodged here, and the rest passed forward 25. leagues to another towne called *la Trinidad* of 15. or 20. households. Here is an hospitall for the poore, and there is none other in all the Island. And they say, that this towne was the greatest in all the Countrie, and that before the Christians came into this land, as a ship passed along the coast, there came in it a very sicke man, which desired the Captaine to set him on shore: and the Captaine did so, and the ship went her way: The sicke man remained set on shore in that countrie, which vntill then had not been haunted by Christians; whereupon the Indians found him, carried him home, and looked vnto him till he was whole; and the Lord of that towne maried him vnto a daughter of his, and had warre with all the inhabitants round about, and by the industrie and valour of the Christian, he subdued and brought vnder his command all the people of that Island. A great while after, the Gouernour *Diego Velasques* went to conquer it, and from thence discouered new *Spaine:* And this Christian which was with the Indians did pacifie them, and brought them to the obedience and subiection of the Gouernour. From this towne *della Trinidad* vnto *Hauana* are 80. leagues without any habitation, which they trauelled. They came to *Hauana* in the end of March; where they found the Gouernor, and the rest of the people which came with him from *Spaine.* The Gouernour sent from *Hauana Iohn Dannusco* with a caruele & two brigantines with 50. men to discouer the hauen of *Florida*; and from thence hee brought

La Trinidad.

Hauana.

men in order, the horſemen in three ſquadrons, the
Vantgard, the Batallion, and the Rerewarde: and ſo
they marched that day, and the day following, com-
paſſing great Creekes which came out of the Bay:
The towne of They came to the towne of *Vcita*, where the Gouer-
Vcita.   nour was, on Sunday the firſt of Iune, being Trinitie
Iune.   Sunday. The towne was of ſeuen or eight houſes. The
Lordes houſe ſtoode neere the ſhore vpon a very hie
mount, made by hand for ſtrength. At another end
of the towne ſtood the Church, and on the top of it
ſtood a fowle made of wood with gilded eies. Heere
Some perles were found ſome pearles of ſmall valew, ſpoiled with
found.   the fire, which the Indians do pierce and ſtring them
like beades, and weare them about their neckes and
handwriſts, and they eſteeme them very much. The
houſes were made of timber, and couered with Palme
leaues. The Gouernour lodged himſelfe in the Lords
houſes, and with him *Vaſques Porcallo*, and *Luys de Moſcoſo*: and in others that were in the middeſt of the
towne, was the chiefe Alcalde or Iuſtice, *Baltaſar de
Gallegos* lodged; and in the ſame houſes was ſet in a
place by it ſelfe, al the prouiſion that came in the ſhips:
the other houſes and the Church were broken down,
and euery three or foure ſouldiers made a little cabin
wherein they lodged. The Countrie round about was
very fennie, and encombred with great and hie trees.
The Gouernor commanded to fel the woods a croſſebow ſhot round about the towne, that the horſes
might runne, and the Chriſtians might haue the aduantage of the Indians, if by chance they ſhould ſet
vpon them by night. In the waies and places conuenient, they had their Centinelles of footemen by two
and two in euery ſtand, which did watch by turnes,
                                                    and

and the horfemen did vifit them, and were readie to af-
fift them, if there were any alarme. The Gouernour
made foure Captaines of the horfemen, and two of the
footemen. The Captaines of the horfemen were, one
of them *Andrew de Vafconcelos*, and another *Pedro Calderan de Badaioz*: and the other two were his kinfemen,
to wit, *Arias Tineco*, and *Alfonfo Romo*, borne likewife
in *Badaioz*. The Captaines of the footemen, the one
was *Francifco Maldonado* of *Salamanca*, and the other
Iuan Rodriguez Lobillo. While wee were in this towne
of *Vcita*, the two Indians, which *Iohn Danufco* had taken on that coaft, and the Gouernor caried along with
him for guides and interpretours, through carelefnes
of two men, which had the charge of them, efcaped a-
way one night. For which the Gouernour and all the
reft were very forie, for they had alreadie made fome
roades, and no Indians could bee taken, becaufe the
countrie was full of marifh grounds, and in many places full of very hie and thicke woods.

Chap. VIII.

*Of fome inrodes that were made into the Countrie: and
how there was a Chriftian found, which had bin long
time in the power of an Indian Lord.*

Rom the towne of *Vcita*, the Gouernour
fent the Alcalde Mayor, *Baltafar de Gallegos*
with 40. horfemen and 80. footemen into the Countrie to fee if they could take
any Indians: and the Captaine *Iohn Rodriguez Lobillo*
another way with 50. footemen, the moft of them
were fwordmen and targettours, and the reft were
fhot and croffebowmen. They paffed through a coun-

trie full of bogges, where horses could not trauell.
Halfe a league from the campe, they lighted vpon cer-
Certaine ca-
bins of In-
dians.
taine cabins of Indians neere a Riuer: The people that
were in them leaped into the Riuer; yet they tooke
foure Indian women : And twentie Indians charged
vs, and so distressed vs, that wee were forced to re-
tire to our campe, being, as they are, exceeding readie with their weapons. It is a people so warlike and
so nimble, that they care not awhit for any footemen.
For if their enemies charge them, they runne away,
and if they turne their backs, they are presently vpon
them. And the thing that they most flee, is the shot of
an arrow. They neuer stand still, but are alwaies running and trauersing from one place to another: by reason whereof neither crossebow nor arcubuse can aime
at them : and before one crossebowman can make one
shot, an Indian will discharge three or foure arrowes;
and he seldome misseth what hee shooteth at. An arrow, where it findeth no armour, pierceth as deepely
as a crossebow. Their bowes are very long, and their
arrowes are made of certaine canes like reedes, very
heauie, & so strong, that a sharpe cane passeth thorow
a target : Some they arme in the point with a sharpe
bone of a fish like a chisel, and in others they fasten certaine stones like points of Diamants. For the most
part when they light vpon an armour, they breake in
the place where they are bound together. Those of
cane do split and pierce a coate of maile, and are more
hurtfull then the other. *Iohn Rodriguez Lobillo* returned to the Campe with sixe men wounded, whereof
one died; and brought the foure Indian women, which
Baltasar Gallegos had taken in the cabins or cotages.
Two leagues from the towne, comming into the
plaine

plaine field, he espied ten or eleuen Indians, among whom was a Christian, which was naked, and scorched with the Sunne, and had his armes razed after the manner of the Indians, and differed nothing at all from them. And assoone as the horsemen saw them they ran toward them. The Indians fled, and some of them hid themselues in a wood, and they ouertooke two or three of them, which were wounded: and the Christian, seeing an horseman runne vpon him with his lance, began to crie out, Sirs, I am a Christian, slay me not, nor these Indians, for they haue saued my life. And straightway he called them, and put them out of feare, and they came foorth of the wood vnto them. The horse men tooke both the Christian and the Indians vp behind them; and toward night came into the Campe with much ioy: which thing being knowne by the Gouernour, and them that remained in the Campe, they were receiued with the like.

Chap. IX.

How this Christian came to the land of Florida, and who he was: and what conference he had with the Gouernour.

His Christians name was *Iohn Ortiz*, and he was borne in *Siuil*, of worshipful parentage. He was 12. yeeres in the hands of the Indians. He came into this Countrie with *Pamphilo de Naruaez*, and returned in the ships to the Island of *Cuba*, where the wife of the Gouernour *Pamphilo de Naruaez* was: and by his commandement with 20. or 30. other in a brigandine returned backe againe to *Florida*: and comming to the port in the sight of

Iohn Ortiz, liued 12. yeeres, among the Floridians of Vcita and Mococo.

D 3   the

the towne, on the shore they saw a cane sticking in the
ground, and riuen at the top, and a letter in it: and they
beleeued that the Gouernour had left it there to giue
aduertisement of himselfe, when he resolued to goe vp
into the land : and they demanded it of foure or fiue
Indians, which walked along the sea shore : and they
bad them by signes to come on shore for it : which a-
gainst the will of the rest *Iohn Ortiz* and another did.
And assoone as they were on land, from the houses of
the towne issued a great number of Indians, which
compassed them about, and tooke them in a place
where they could not flee: and the other which sought
to defend himselfe, they presentlie killed vpon the
place, and tooke *Iohn Ortiz* aliue, and carried him to
Vcita their Lord. And those of the brigandine sought
not to land, but put themselues to sea, and returned to
the Island of *Cuba. Vcita* commanded to bind *Iohn*
Ortiz hand and foote vpon foure stakes aloft vpon a
raft, and to make a fire vnder him, that there he might
bee burned : But a daughter of his desired him that he
would not put him to death, alleaging, that one only
Christian could do him neither hurt nor good, telling
him, that it was more for his honour to keepe him as a
captiue. And *Vcita* granted her request, and commanded him to be cured of his wounds : and assoone as he
was whole, he gaue him the charge of the keeping of
the Temple : because that by night the wolues did
cary away the dead corpses out of the same: who com-
mended himselfe to God and tooke vpon him the
charge of his temple. One night the wolues gate from
him the corpes of a little child, the sonne of a principal
Indian ; and going after them he threw a darte at one
of the wolues and strooke him that carried away the

corps,

corps, who feeling himfelfe wounded, left it, and fell
downe dead neere the place : and hee not woting
what he had done, becaufe it was night, went backe a-
gaine to the Temple : the morning being come, and
finding not the bodie of the child, he was very fad. Affoone as *Vcita* knew thereof, he refolued to put him to
death ; and fent by the tract, which he faid the wolues
went, and found the bodie of the child, and the wolfe
dead a little beyond : whereat *Vcita* was much contented with the Chriftian, and with the watch which hee
kept in the Temple, and from thence forward efteemed him much. Three yeeres after hee fell into his
hands, there came another Lord, called *Mococo*, who
dwelleth two daies iourny from the Port, and burned
his towne. *Vcita* fled to another towne that he had in
another fea port. Thus *Iohn Ortiz* loft his office and fauour that he had with him. Thefe people being wor-
fhippers of the diuell, are wont to offer vp vnto him
the liues and blood of their Indians, or of any other
people they can come by : and they report, that when
he will haue them doe that facrifice vnto him, he fpea-
keth with them, and telleth them that he is athirft, and
willeth them to facrifice vnto him. *Iohn Ortiz* had notice by the damfell that had deliuered him from ỹ fire,
how her father was determined to facrifice him ỹ day
following, who willed him to flee to *Mococo* : for fhee
knew ỹ he would vfe him wel: for fhe heard fay, that he
had asked for him, and faid hee would bee glad to fee
him : and becaufe he knew not the way, fhe went with
him halfe a league out of the towne by night, and fet
him in the way, & returned, becaufe fhe would not be
difcouered. *Iohn Ortiz* trauailed all that night, and by
ỹ morning came vnto a Riuer, which is in the territorie

of

Mococo
dwelleth two
daies iournie
from Vcita.

A Riuer.

of *Mocoço*: and there he saw two Indians fishing, and
becaufe they were in war with the people of *Vcita*, and
their languages were different, and hee knew not the
láguage of *Mocoço*, he was afraid, becaufe he could not
tell them who hee was, nor how hee came thither, nor
was able to anfwer any thing for himfelfe, that they
would kill him, taking him for one of the Indians of
Vcita, and before they efpied him, he came to the place
where they had laid their weapons : & affoone as they
faw him, they fled toward the towne, and although he
willed thé to ftay, becaufe he meant to do thé no hurt,
yet they vnderftood him not, and ran away as faft as e-
uer they could. And affone as they came to the towne
with great outcries, many Indians came forth againft
him, and began to compaffe him to fhoote at him: *Iohn
Ortiz* feeing himfelfe in fo great danger, fheilded himfelfe with certaine trees, and began to fhreeke out, and
crie very loud, and to tell them that he was a Chriftian,
and that he was fled from *Vcita*, and was come to fee
and ferue *Mocoço* his Lord. It pleafed God that at that
very inftant there came thither an Indian that could
fpeake the language and vnderftood him ; and pacified the reft ; who told them what hee faid. Then ran
from thence three or foure Indians to beare the newes
to their Lord : who came foorth a quarter of a league
from the towne to receiue him ; and was very glad of
him. He caufed him prefently to fweare according to
the cuftome of the Chriftians, that hee would not run
away from him to any other Lord : and promifed him
to entreate him very well ; and that if at any time there
came any Chriftians into that countrie, he would freely let him goe, and giue him leaue to goe to them: and
likewife tooke his oth to performe the fame according
　　　　　　　　　　　　　　　　　　　　　　to

to the Indian cuſtome. About three yeeres after certaine Indians, which were fiſhing at ſea two leagues
from the towne, brought newes to *Mocoço* that they
had ſeene ſhips: and hee called *Iohn Ortiz*, and gaue
him leaue to go his way: who taking his leaue of him,
with all the haſte he could came to the ſea, and finding
no ſhips, he thought it to be ſome deceit, and that the
Cacique had done the ſame to learne his mind. So he
dwelt with *Mocoço* nine yeeres, with ſmall hope of ſeeing any Chriſtians. Aſſoone as our Gouernor arriued
in *Florida*, it was knowne to *Mocoço*, & ſtraightway he
ſignified to *Iohn Ortiz*, that Chriſtians were lodged in
the towne of *Vcita*: And he thought he had ieſted with
him, as hee had done before, and told him, that by this
time he had forgotten the Chriſtians, and thought of
nothing elſe but to ſerue him. But he aſſured him that
it was ſo, and gaue him licence to goe vnto them : ſaying vnto him, that if hee would not doe it, and if the
Chriſtians ſhould goe their way, he ſhould not blame
him, for hee had fulfilled that which he had promiſed
him. The ioy of *Iohn Ortiz* was ſo great, that hee could
not beleeue that it was true : notwithſtanding he gaue
him thankes, and tooke his leaue of him : and *Mocoço*
gaue him tenne or eleuen principall Indians to beare
him companie : and as they went to the port where
the Gouernour was, they met with *Baltaſar de Gallegos*,
as I haue declared before. Aſſoone as he was come to
the campe, the Gouernour commanded to giue him
a ſute of apparrell, and very good armour, and a faire
horſe; and enquired of him, whether hee had notice
of any countrie, where there was any gold or ſiluer?
He anſwered, No, becauſe he neuer went ten leagues
compaſſe from the place where he dwelt : But that

Mocoço his towne within 2. leagues of the ſea.

E   30.

Paracossi 30. leagues from Puerto de Spirito Santo.

30. leagues from thence dwelt an Indian Lord, which was called *Parocossi*, to whom *Mocoço* and *Vcita*, with al the rest of that coast paied tribute, and that hee peraduenture might haue notice of some good countrie: and that his land was better then that of the sea coast, and more fruitfull and plentifull of maiz. Whereof the Gouernour receiued great contentment: and said that he desired no more then to finde victuals, that hee might goe into the maine land, for the land of *Florida*, was so large, that in one place or other there could not chuse but bee some rich Countrie. The *Cacique Mocoço* came to the Port to visit the Gouernor, and made this speech following.

Right hie and mightie Lord, I being lesser in mine owne conceit for to obey you, then any of those which you haue vnder your command; and greater in desire to doe you greater seruices, doe appeare before your Lordship with so much confidence of receiuing fauour, as if in effect this my good will were manifested vnto you in workes: not for the small seruice I did vnto you touching the Christian which I had in my power, in giuing him freely his libertie, (For I was bound to doe it to preserue mine honour, and that which I had promised him:) but because it is the part of great men to vse great magnificences: And I am perswaded, that as in bodily perfections, and commanding of good people, you doe exceede all men in the world, so likewise you doe in the parts of the minde, in which you may boast of the bountie of nature. The fauour which I hope for of your Lordship is, that you would hold mee for yours, and bethinke your selfe to command me any thing, wherein I may doe you seruice.

The Gouernour answered him, That although in freeing and sending him the Christian, he had preserued his honour and promise, yet he thanked him, and held

held it in such esteeme, as it had no comparison; and that hee would alwaies hold him as his brother, and would fauour him in all things to the vtmost of his power. Then he commanded a shirt to be giuen him, and other things, wherewith the Cacique being verie well contented, tooke his leaue of him, aud departed to his owne towne.

Chap. X.

How the Gouernour sent the ships to Cuba: *and left an hundred men at the Hauen* de Spirito Santo, *and himself with the rest of his people went into the maine land.*

Rom the Port *de Spirito Santo* where the Gouernour lay, he sent the Alcalde Mayor *Baltasar de Gallégos* with 50. horsemen, and 30. or 40. footemen to the prouince of *Paracossi,* to view the disposition of the countrie, and enforme himselfe of the land farther inward, and to send him word of such things as he found. Likewise he sent his shippes backe to the Island of *Cuba,* that they might returne within a certaine time with victuals. *Vasques Porcallo de figueroa,* which went with the Gouernour as Captaine Generall, (whose principall intent was to send slaues from *Florida,* to the Island of *Cuba,* where he had his goods and mines,) hauing made some inrodes, and seeing no Indians were to be got, because of the great bogs and thicke woods ỹ were in the Countrie, considering the disposition of the same, determined to returne to *Cuba.* And though there was some difference between him & the Gouernor, whereupon they neither dealt nor conuersed together with good

coun-

countenance, yet notwithstanding with louing words he asked him leaue and departed from him. *Baltasar de Gallegos* came to the *Paracossi*: There came to him 30. Indians from the Cacique, which was absent from his towne, and one of them made this speech:

Paracossi, the Lord of this prouince, whose vassals we are, sendeth vs vnto your worship, to know what it is that you seeke in this his Countrie, and wherein he may doe you seruice.

Baltasar de Gallegos said vnto him, that hee thanked them very much for their offer, willing them to warne their Lord to come to his towne, and that there they would talke and confirme their peace and friendship, which he much desired. The Indians went their way, and returned the next day, and said, that their Lord was ill at ease, and therefore could not come, but that they came on his behalfe to see what he demanded. He asked them if they knew or had notice of any rich Countrie where there was gold or siluer. They told them, they did: and that toward the West, there was a Prouince which was called *Cale*; and that others that inhabited other Countries had warre with the people of that Countrie, where the most part of the yeere was sommer, and that there was much gold: and that when those their enemies came to make warre with them of *Cale*, these inhabitants of *Cale* did weare hats of gold, in manner of head peeces. *Baltasar de Gallegos*, seeing that the Cacique came not, thinking all that they said was fained, with intent that in the meane time they might set themselues in safetie, fearing, that if he did let them goe, they would returne no more, commanded the thirty Indians to be chained, and sent word to the Gouernour, by eight horsemen, what had passed: whereof the Gouernour with al that were with him, at the Port

de

de Spirito Santo receiued great comfort, suppoſing, that that which the Indians reported, might be true. Hee left Captaine *Calderan* at the Port, with thirtie horſemen, and ſeuentie footemen, with prouiſion for two yeeres, and himſelfe with all the reſt marched into the maine land, and came to the *Paracoſſi*, at whoſe Paracoſſi. towne *Baltaſar de Gallegos* was : and from thence with all his men tooke the way to *Cale.* He paſſed by a little towne, called *Acela,* and came to another, called Acela. *Tocaſte* : and from thence hee went before with 30. Tocaſte. horſemen, and 50. footemen toward *Cale.* And paſ- Another ſing by a towne, whence the people were fled, they towne. ſaw Indians a little from thence in a lake, to whom the A Lake. Interpretour ſpake. They came vnto them and gaue them an Indian for a guide : and hee came to a Riuer A ſwift Riuer. with a great current, and vpon a tree, which was in the midſt of it, was made a bridge, whereon the men paſ- ſed : the horſes ſwam ouer by a hawſer, that they were pulled by from the otherſide : for one, which they droue in at the firſt without it, was drowned. From thence the Gouernour ſent two horſemen to his people that were behind, to make haſte after him ; becauſe the way grew long, and their victuals ſhort. Hee came to *Cale,* and found the towne without peo- Cale. ple. He tooke three Indians which were ſpies, and tar- ried there for his people that came after, which were ſore vexed with hunger and euill waies, becauſe the Countrie was very barren of Maiz, low, and full of wa- ter, bogs, and thicke woods ; and the victuals, which they brought with them from the Port *de Spirito Santo,* were ſpent. Whereſoeuer any towne was found, there were ſome beetes, and hee that came firſt gathered them, and ſodden with water and ſalt, did eate them

E 3   with-

without any other thing : and such as could not get them, gathered the stalkes of Maiz and eate them, which because they were young had no Maiz in them. when they came to the Riuer which the Gouernour had passed, they found palmitos vpon low Palmetrees like those of *Andaluzia.* There they met with the two horsemen which the Gouernour sent vnto them, and they brought newes that in *Cale* there was plentie of Maiz ; at which newes they all reioyced. Assoone as they came to *Cale*, the Gouernour commanded them to gather all the Maiz that was ripe in the field, which was sufficient for three moneths. At the gathering of it the Indians killed three Christians, and one of them which were taken told the Gouernour, that within seuen daies iournie, there was a very great Prouince, and plentifull of Maiz, which was called *Apalache*. And presently hee departed from *Cale* with 50. horsemen, and 60. footemen. He left the master of the Campe *Luys de Moscoso* with all the rest of the people there, with charge that hee should not depart thence vntill he had word from him. And because hitherto none had gotten any slaues, the bread that euery one was to eate, he was faine himselfe to beate in a morter made in a peece of timber with a pestle, and some of them did sift the flower through their shirts of maile. They baked their bread vpon certaine tileshares which they set ouer the fire, in such sort as heretofore I haue said they vse to doe in *Cuba*. It is so troublesome to grind their Maiz, that there were many that would rather not eate it, then grind it : and did eate the Maiz parched and sodden.

CHAP.

Chap. XI.

How the Gouernour came to Caliquen, *and carrying from thence the Cacique with him went to* Napetuca, *where the Indians fought to haue taken him from him, and in an affault many of them were flaine, and taken prifoners.*

He 11. day of August 1539. the Gouernour departed from *Cale*; hee lodged in a little town called *Ytara*, and the next day in another called *Potano*, and the third day at *Vtinama*, and came to another towne, which they named the towne of *E-uil peace*; becaufe an Indian came in peace, faying, That he was the Cacique, and that he with his people would ferue the Gouernour, and that if he would fet free 28. perfons, men and women, which his men had taken the night before, he would command prouifion to be brought him, and would giue him a guide to inftruct him in his way: The Gouernour commanded them to be fet at libertie, and to keepe him in fafegard. The next day in the morning there came many Indians, and fet themfelues round about the towne neere to a wood. The Indian wifhed them to carrie him neere them; and that he would fpeake vnto them, and affure them, and that they would doe whatfoeuer hee commanded them. And when he faw himfelfe neere vnto them he brake from them, and ran away fo fwiftly from the Chriftians, that there was none that could ouertake him, and all of them fled into the woods. The Gouernour commanded to loofe a grayhound, which

was

Ytara.

Potano.
Vtinama.

The towne of
Euill peace.

was alreadie fleshed on them, which passing by many other Indians, caught the counterfait Cacique, which had escaped from the Christians, and held him till they came to take him. From thence the Gouernour lodged at a towne called *Cholupaha:* and because it had store of Maiz in it, they named it *Villa farta.* Beyond the same there was a Riuer, on which he made a bridge of timber, and trauelled two daies through a desert. The 17. of August, he came to *Caliquen,* where he was informed of the Prouince of *Apalache:* They told him that *Pamphilo de Naruaez* had bin there, and that there hee tooke shipping, because hee could find no way to goe forward: That there was none other towne at al, but that on both sides was all water. The whole companie were very sad for these newes; and counselled the Gouernour to goe backe to the Port *de Spirito Santo,* and to abandon the Countrie of *Florida,* lest hee should perish as *Naruaez* had done: declaring, that if he went forward, hee could not returne backe when he would, and that the Indians would gather vp that small quantitie of Maiz which was left. Whereunto the Gouernour answered, that he would not go backe, till he had seene with his eies that which they reported: saying, that he could not beleeue it, and that wee should be put out of doubt before it were long. And he sent to *Luys de Moscoso* to come presently from *Cale,* and that he tarried for him here. *Luys de Moscoso* and many others thought, that from *Apalache* they should returne backe; and in *Cale* they buried their yron tooles, and diuers other things. They came to *Caliquen* with great trouble; because the Countrie, which the Gouernor had passed by, was spoiled and destitute of Maiz. After all the people were come together, hee com-

Cholupaha.

A Riuer.

Caliquen.

commanded a bridge to bee made ouer a Riuer that A Riuer.
passed neere the towne. Hee departed from *Caliquen*
the 10. of September, and carried the Cacique with
him. After hee had trauelled three daies, there came
Indians peaceably, to visit their Lord, and euery day
met vs on the way playing vpon flutes : which is a token that they vse, that men may know that they come
in peace. They said, that in our way before there was a
Cacique, whose name was *Vzachil*, a kinseman of the
Cacique of *Caliquen* their Lord, waiting for him with
many presents, and they desired the Gouernor that he
would loose the Cacique. But he would not, fearing
that they would rise, and would not giue him any
guides, & sent them away from day to day with good
words. He trauelled fiue daies, he passed by some smal Some small townes.
townes, he came to a towne called *Napetuca*, the 15. day
of September. Thither came 14. or 15. Indians, and Napetuca.
besought y Gouernor to let loose the Cacique of *Ca-*
liquen their Lord. He answered them that he held him
not in prison, but that hee would haue him to accompanie him to *Vzachil*. The Gouernour had notice by
Iohn Ortiz, that an Indian told him how they determined to gather themselues together, and come vpon
him, and giue him battell, and take away the Cacique
from him. The day that it was agreed vpon, the Gouernour commanded his men to bee in a readines, and
that the horsemen should bee readie armed and on
horsebacke euery one in his lodging, because the Indians might not see them, and so more confidently come
to the towne. There came foure hundred Indians in
sight of the campe with their bowes and arrowes, and
placed themselues in a wood, and sent two Indians to
bid the Gouernour to deliuer them the Cacique. The

F   Gouernour

Gouernour with sixe footemen, leading the Cacique
by the hand, and talking with him, to secure the Indians, went toward the place where they were: And seeing a fit time, commanded to sound a trumpet: and
presently those that were in the towne in the houses,
both horse and foot, set vpon the Indians, which were
so suddenly assaulted, that the greatest care they had
was which way they should flee: They killed two horses; one was the Gouernours, and hee was presently
horsed againe vpon another. There were 30. or 40.
Indians slaine. The rest fled to two very great lakes,
that were somewhat distant the one from the other:
There they were swimming, and the Christians round
about them. The calieuermen and crossebowmen shot
at them from the banke; but the distance being great,
and shooting afarre off, they did them no hurt. The
Gouernour commanded that the same night they
should compasse one of the lakes, because they were so
great, that there were not mé enow to compasse them
both: being beset, assoone as night shut in, the Indians,
with determination to runne away, came swimming
very softly to the banke; and to hide themselues, they
put a water lillie leafe on their heads. The horsemen assoone as they perceiued it to stirre, ran into the water
to the horses breasts, and the Indians fled againe into
the lake. So this night passed without any rest on both
sides. *Iohn Ortiz* perswaded them, that seeing they
could not escape, they should yeeld themselues to the
Gouernour: which they did, enforced thereunto by
the coldnes of the water; and one by one, hee first
whom the cold did first ouercome, cried to *Iohn Ortiz,*
desiring that they would not kill him; for hee came to
put himselfe into the hands of the Gouernour. By the
morning

Two very
great lakes.

morning watch they made an end of yeelding themselues : only 12. principall men, being more honora-
ble and valorous then the reſt, reſolued rather to die
then to come into his hands. And the Indians of *Para-*
coſſi, which were now looſed out of chaines, went
ſwimming to them, and pulled them out by the haire
of their heads, and they were all put in chaines ; and
the next day were diuided among the Chriſtians for
their ſeruice. Being thus in captiuitie, they determined to rebell ; and gaue in charge to an Indian, which
was interpretour, and held to be valiant, that aſſoone
as the Gouernour did come to ſpeake with him, hee
ſhould caſt his hands about his necke, and choke him:
Who, whē he ſaw opportunitie, laid hands on the Gouernour, and before he caſt his hands about his necke,
he gaue him ſuch a blow on the noſtrils, that hee made
them guſh out with blood, and preſently all the reſt
did riſe. He that could get any weapons at hand, or
the handle wherewith he did grind the Maiz, ſought
to kill his maſter, or the firſt hee met before him : and
hee that could get a lance or ſword at hand, beſtirred
himſelfe in ſuch ſort with it, as though he had vſed it
all his life time. One Indian in the market place enclo-
ſed betweene 15. or 20. footemen, made a way like a
bull with a ſword in his hand, till certaine halbardiers
of the Gouernour came, which killed him. Another
gat vp with a lance to a loft made of canes, which they
build to keepe their Maiz in, which they call a Barba-
coa, and there hee made ſuch a noiſe, as though tenne
men had been there defending the doore : they ſlew
him with a partiſan. The Indians were in all about two
hundred men. They were all ſubdued. And ſome of
the youngeſt the Gouernour gaue to them which had

Marginal notes: A new conſpiracie. Two hundred Indians taken.

good

good chaines, and were carefull to looke to them that they gat not away. Al the rest he commanded to be put to death, being tied to a stake in the midst of the market place: and the Indians of the *Paracossi* did shoote them to death.

CHAP. XII.

How the Gouernour came to Apalache, *and was informed, that within the land, there was much gold.*

A Riuer.

He Gouernour departed from *Napetuca* the 23. of September: he lodged by a Riuer, where two Indians brought him a buck from the Cacique of *Vzachil.* The next day he passed by a great towne called *Hapaluya*; and lodged at *Vzachil*, and found no people in it, because they durst not tarrie for the notice the Indians had of the slaughter of *Napetuca.* He found in that towne great store of Maiz, french beanes, and *pompions, which is their foode, and that wherewith the Christians there sustained themselues. The Maiz is like course millet, and the pompions are better and more sauorie then those of *Spaine.* From thence the Gouernour sent two Captaines each a sundry way to seeke the Indians. They tooke an hundred men and women: of which aswel there as in other places where they made any inrodes, the Captaine chose one or two for the Gouernour, and diuided the rest to himselfe, and those that went with him. They led these Indians in chaines with yron collars about their neckes; and they serued to carrie their stuffe, and to grind their Maiz, and for other seruices that such captiues could doe. Sometimes it happened that going for wood or

Maiz.

Hapaluya a great towne.
Vzachil.

* Aboboras.

Maiz with them, they killed the Christian that led them, and ran away with the chaine: others filed their chaines by night with a peece of stone, wherewith they cut them, and vse it in stead of yron. Those that were perceiued paid for themselues, and for the rest, because they should not dare to doe the like another time. The women and young boyes, when they were once an hundred leagues from their Countrie, and had forgotten things, they let goe loose, and so they serued; and in a very short space they vnderstood the language of the Christians. From *Vzachil* the Gouernour departed toward *Apalache*, and in two daies iournie, hee came to a towne called *Axille*, and from Axille. thence forward the Indians were carelesse, because they had as yet no notice of the Christians. The next day in the morning, the first of October, he departed A Riuer. from thence, and commanded a bridge to bee made ouer a Riuer which hee was to passe. The deepe of the Riuer where the bridge was made, was a stones cast, and forward a crossebow shot the water came to the waste; and the wood, whereby the Indians came to see if they could defend the passage, and disturbe those which made the bridge, was very hie and thicke. The crossebow men so bestirred themselues that they made them giue back: and certain plancks were cast into the Riuer, whereon the men passed, which made good the passage. The Gouernor passed vpõ Wednesday, which was S. *Francis* his day, and lodged at a towne which was called *Vitachuco*, subiect to *Apalache*: he found it Vitachuco. burning; for the Indians had set it on fire. From thence forward the countrie was much inhabited, and had great store of Maiz. Hee passed by many granges like hamlets. On Sunday the 25. of October, he came October 25.

F 3   to

Vzela.

Anaica Apalache.

to a towne, which is called *Vzela*, and vpon Tuesday to *Anaica Apalache*, where the Lord of all that Countrie and Prouince was resident : in which towne the Campemaster, whose office it is to quarter out, and lodge men, did lodge all the companie round about within a league, and halfe a league of it. There were other townes, where was great store of Maiz, Pompions, French Beanes, and Plummes of the Countrie, which are better then those of *Spaine,* and they grow in the fields without planting. The victuals that were thought necessarie to passe the winter, were gathered from these townes to *Anaica Apalache.* The Gouernour was informed, that the sea was ten leagues from thence. Hee presently sent a Captaine thither with horsemen and footemen : And sixe leagues on the way, he found a towne, which was named *Ochete*, and so came to the sea; and found a great tree felled, and cut into peeces, with stakes set vp like mangers, and saw the skulles of horses. Hee returned with this newes. And that was held for certaine, which was reported of *Pamphilo de Naruaez*, that there hee had builded the barkes wherewith he went out of the land of *Florida*, and was cast away at Sea. Presently the Gouernour sent *Iohn Danusco* with 30. horsemen to the port *de Spiritu Santo*, where *Calderan* was, with order, that they should abandon the port, and all of them come to *Apalache.* He departed on Saturday the 17. of Nouember. In *Vzachit* and other townes that stood in the way he found great store of people alreadie carelesse. Hee would take none of the Indians, for not hindring himselfe, because it behooued him to giue them no leasure to gather themselues together. He passed through the townes by night, and rested without the townes three

or

Apalache within 10. leagues of the sea.

Ochete.
The sea.

or foure houres. In tenne daies he came to the Port
de Spirito Santo. He carried with him 20. Indian women, which he tooke in *Ytara*, and *Potano*, neere vnto
Cale, and sent them to *Donna Isabella* in the two cara-
uels, which hee sent from the Port *de Svirito Santo* to
Cuba. And he carried all the footemen in the brigandines and coasting along the shore, came to *Apalache*.
And *Calderan* with the horsemen, and some crossebowmen on foote went by land; and in some places
the Indians set vpon him, and wounded some of his
men. Assoone as he came to *Apalache*; presently the
Gouernour sent sawed plankes and spikes to the sea-
side, wherewith was made a piragna or barke, wherein
were embarked 30. men well armed; which went out
of the Bay to the Sea, looking for the brigandines.
Sometimes they fought with the Indians, which passed along the harbour in their canoes. Vpon Saturday the 29. of Nouember, there came an Indian
through the Watch vndiscouered, and set the towne
on fire, and with the great wind that blew, two parts of
it were consumed in a short time. On Sonday the 28. of
December came *Iohn Danusco* with the brigandines.
The Gouernour sent *Francisco Maldonado* a Captaine
of footemen with 50. men to discouer the coast Westward, and to seeke some Port, because he had determined to go by land, and discouer ý part. That day there
went out eight horsemen by commandement of the
Gouernor into the field, two leagues about the towne
to seeke Indians : for they were now so emboldened,
that within two crossebow shot of ý camp, they came
and slew men. They found two men and a woman gathering French Beanes : the men, though they might
haue fled, yet because they would not leaue the woman,

The Port de
Spiritu Santo
tenne daies
iou:n'e from
Apalache.

Nouem.29.

Decem.28.

man, which was one of their wiues, they resolued to die fighting : and before they were slaine, they wounded three horses, whereof one died within a few daies after. *Calderan* going with his men by the Sea-coast, from a wood that was neere the place, the Indians set vpon him, and made him forsake his way, and many of them that went with him forsooke some necessarie victuals, which they carried with them. Three or foure daies after the limited time giuen by the Gouernour to *Maldonado* for his going and comming, being alreadie determined and resolued, if within eight daies he did not come, to tarrie no longer for him, he came, and brought an Indian from a Prouince, which was called *Ochus*, sixtie leagues Westward from *Apalache*; where he had found a good Port of good depth and defense against weather. And because the Gouernor hoped to find a good countrie forward, he was very well contented. And he sent *Maldonado* for victuals to *Hauana*, with order, that he should tarrie for him at the Port of *Ochus*, which hee had discouered, for hee would goe seeke it by land : and if he should chance to stay, and not come thither that summer, that then hee should returne to *Hauana*, and should come againe the next summer after, and tarrie for him at that port : for hee said hee would doe none other thing but goe to seeke *Ochus*. *Francisco Maldonado* departed, and in his place for Captaine of the footemen remained *Iohn de Guzman*. Of those Indians which were taken in *Napetuca*, the treasurer *Iohn Gaytan* had a young man, which said, that he was not of that Countrie, but of another farre off toward the Sunrising, and that it was long since he had trauelled to see Countries; and that his Countrie was called *Yupaha*, and that a woman did gouerne

Ochus 60. leagues West of Apalache.

Chap. 11.

gouerne it: and that the towne where she was resident „
was of a wonderfull bignesse, and that many Lords „
round about were tributaries to her: and some gaue „
her clothes, and others gold in abundance: and hee Abundance
told, how it was taken out of the mines, and was moul- of gold.
ten and refined, as if hee had seene it done, or the diuel „
had taught it him. So that all those which knew any „
thing concerning the same, said that it was impossible „
to giue so good a relation, without hauing seene it:
And all of them, as if they had seene it, by the signes
that he gaue, beleeued all that he said to be true.

CHAP. XIII.
How the Gouernour departed from Apalache *to seeke*
Yupaha, *and of that which happened vnto him.*

 N Wedensday the third of March, of the March the 3.
yeere 1540. the Gouernor departed from 1540.
Anaica Apalache to seeke *Yupaha.* He commanded his men to goe prouided with
Maiz for sixtie leagues of desert. The horsemen carried their Maiz on their horses, and the footemen at
their sides: because the Indians that were for seruice,
with their miserable life that they lead that winter, being naked and in chaines, died for the most part. With- A great Riuer.
in foure daies iournie they came to a great Riuer: and
they made a piragua or ferrie bote, and because of the
great current, they made a cable with chaines, which
they fastened on both sides of the Riuer; and the ferrie bote went along by it; and the horses swam ouer,
being drawne with capstans. Hauing passed the Riuer,
in a day and an halfe, they came to a towne called *Ca-* Capachiqui.
pachiqui. Vpon Friday, the 11. of March, they found

Indians in armes. The next day fiue Christians went
to seeke morters, which the Indians haue to beate their
Maiz, and they went to certaine houses on the back-
side of the Campe enuironed with a wood: And within the wood were many Indians which came to spie
vs; of the which came other fiue and set vpon vs. One
of the Christians came running away, giuing an a-
larme vnto the Campe. Those which were most readie
answered the alarme. They found one Christian dead,
and three sore wounded. The Indians fled vnto a lake
adioyning neere a very thicke wood, where the horses
could not enter. The Gouernour departed from *Ca-*
pachiqui, and passed through a desert. On Wednesday
the 21. of the moneth he came to a towne called *To-*
alli : And from thence forward there was a difference
in the houses. For those which were behind vs were

Toalli.   thatched with straw, and those of *Toalli* were couered
with reeds, in manner of tiles. These houses are verie
cleanly. Some of them had walles daubed with clay,
which shewed like a mudwall. In all the cold Countrie the Indians haue euery one a house for the winter
daubed with clay within and without, and the doore
is very little : they shut it by night, and make fire within; so that they are in it as warme as in a stoue : and so
it continueth all night that they need not clothes : and
besides these, they haue others for summer; and their
kitchins neere them, where they make fire and bake
their bread : and they haue barbacoas wherein they
keepe their Maiz; which is an house set vp in the aire
vpon foure stakes, boorded about like a chamber, and
the floore of it is of cane hurdles. The differēce which
Lords or principall mens houses haue from the rest,
besides they be greater, is, that they haue great galleries

ries in their fronts, and vnder them seates made of canes in manner of benches : and round about them they haue many lofts, wherein they lay vp that which the Indians doe giue them for tribute, which is Maiz, Deeres skins, and mantles of the Countrie, which are like blankets: they make them of the inner rinde of the barkes of trees, and some of a kind of grasse like vnto nettles, which being beaten, is like vnto flaxe. The wo- men couer themselues with these mantles; they put one about them from the wast downeward; and ano- ther ouer their shoulder, with their right arme out, like vnto the Egyptians. The men weare but one mantle vpon their shoulders after the same manner : and haue their secrets hid with a Deeres skin, made like a linen breech, which was wont to be vsed in *Spaine.* The skins are well corried, and they giue them what colour they list, so perfect, that if it be red, it seemeth a very fine cloth in graine, and the blacke is most fine : and of the same leather they make shooes; and they die their man- tles in the same colours. The Gouernour departed from *Toalli* the 24. of March : he came on Thursday at euening to a small Riuer, where a bridge was made whereon the people passed, and *Benit Fernandez* a Por- tugall fell off from it, and was drowned. Assoone as the Gouernour had passed the Riuer, a little distance thence he found a towne called *Achese.* The Indians had no notice of the Christians : they leaped into a Riuer : some men and women were taken; among which was one that vnderstood the youth which gui- ded the Gouernour to *Yupaha :* whereby that which he had reported was more confirmed. For they had passed through Countries of diuers languages, and some which he vnderstood not. The Gouernour sent

A grasse like flaxe.

Excellent colours.

A small Riuer.

Achese.

by one of the Indians that were taken to call the Cacique, which was on the other side of the Riuer. Hee
came and made this speech following:

Right high, right mightie, and excellent Lord, those things
which seldome happen doe cause admiration. What then may
the sight of your Lordship, and your people doe to mee and
mine, whom we neuer saw? especially being mounted on such
fierce beasts as your horses are, entring with such violence
and furie into my Countrie, without my knowledge of your
comming. It was a thing so strange, and caused such feare
and terrour in our mindes, that it was not in our power to
stay and receiue your Lordship with the solemnitie due to so
high and renowned a Prince, as your Lordship is. And tru-
sting in your greatnesse and singular vertues, I doe not onely
hope to be freed from blame, but also to receiue fauours: and
the first which I demand of your Lordship is, that you will vse
me, my Countrie, and subiects as your owne: and the second,
that you will tell mee who you are, and whence you come, and
whither you goe, aud what you seeke: that I the better may
serue you therein.

The Gouernour answered him, that hee thanked
him as much for his offer and good will, as if hee had
receiued it, and as if hee had offered him a great treasure: and told him that he was the sonne of the Sun,
and came from those parts where he dwelt, and trauelled through that Countrie, and sought the greatest
Lord, and richest Prouince that was in it. The Cacique told him; that farther forward dwelt a great Lord,
and that his dominion was calle *Ocute*. He gaue him a
guide, and an interpretour for that Prouince. The Gouernour commanded his Indians to bee set free, and
A Riuer very　trauelled through his Countrie vp a Riuer very well
well inhabi-　inhabited. He departed from his towne the first of A-
ted.
　　　　　　　　　　　　　　　　　　　　　　prill;

prill; and left a very high croſſe of Wood ſet vp in the
middeſt of the market place : and becauſe the time
gaue no more leaſure, hee declared to him onely, that
that croſſe was a memorie of ỹ ſame, whereon Chriſt,
which was God and man, and created the heauens
and the earth, ſuffered for our ſaluation : therefore he
exhorted them that they ſhould reuerence it : and they
made ſhew as though they would doe ſo. The fourth
of Aprill the Gouernour paſſed by a towne called *Al-*
tamaca, and the 10. of the moneth he came to *Ocute.*
The Cacique ſent him two thouſand Indians with a
preſent, to wit, many conies, and partriges, bread of
Maiz, two hens, and many dogs : which among the
Chriſtians were eſteemed as if they had been fat we-
thers, becauſe of the great want of fleſh meate and ſalt,
and hereof in many places, and many times was great
need; and they were ſo ſcarſe, that if a man fell ſicke,
there was nothing to cheriſh him withall : and with a
ſickneſſe, that in another place eaſilie might haue been
remedied, he conſumed away till nothing but skinne
and bones were left : and they died of pure weaknes,
ſome of them ſaying, If I had a ſlice of meate, or a few
cornes of ſalt, I ſhould not die. The Indians want no
fleſhmeat : for they kill with their arrowes many
deere, hennes, conies, and other wild fowle : for they
are very cunning at it : which skill the Chriſtians had
not : and though they had it, they had no leaſure to
vſe it : for the moſt of the time they ſpent in trauell,
and durſt not preſume to ſtraggle aſide. And becauſe
they were thus ſcanted of fleſh, when ſixe hundred
men that went with *Soto*, came to any towne, and
found 30. or 40. dogs, he that could get one and kill it,
thought himſelfe no ſmall man : and he that killed it,

Altamaca.

Ocute.

Conics, Patri-
ges, Hens,
Dogges.

and

and gaue not his Captaine one quarter, if he knew it, he frowned on him, and made him feele it, in the watches, or in any other matter of labour that was offered, wherein hee might doe him a displeasure. On Monday the 12. of Aprill, the Gouernour departed from *Ocute*: The Cacique gaue him two hundred *Tamenes*, to wit, Indians to carrie burdens: hee passed through a towne, the Lord whereof was named *Cofaqui*, and came to a prouince of an Indian Lord, called *Patofa*, who, because he was in peace with the Lord of *Ocute*, and with the other bordering Lords, had many daies before notice of the Gouernour, and desired to see him: He came to visit him, and made this speech following.

Cofaqui.

Patofa.

Mightie Lord, now with good reason I will craue of fortune to requite this my so great prosperitie with some small aduersitie; and I will count my selfe verie rich, seeing I haue obtained that, which in this world I most desired, which is, to see, and bee able to doe your Lordship some seruice. And although the tongue bee the image of that which is in the heart, and that the contentment which I feele in my heart I cannot dissemble, yet is it not sufficient wholly to manifest the same. Where did this your Countrie, which I doe gouerne, deserue to be visited of so soueraigne, and so excellent a Prince, whom all the rest of the world ought to obey and serue? And those which inhabit it being so base, what shall bee the issue of such happines, if their memorie doe not represent vnto them some aduersitie that may betide them, according to the order of fortune? If from this day forward we may be capable of this benefit, that your Lordship will hold vs for your owne, we cannot faile to be fauoured and maintained in true iustice and reason, and to haue the name of men. For such as are void of reason and iustice, may bee compared to brute beasts. For

mine

mine owne part, from my very heart with reuerence due to such a Prince, I offer my selfe vnto your Lordship, & beseech you; that in reward of this my true good will, you will vouchsafe to make vse of mine owne person, my Countrie, and subiects.

The Gouernour answered him, that his offers and good wil declared by the effect, did highly please him, whereof he would alwaies be mindfull to honour and fauour him as his brother. This Countrie, from the first peaceable Cacique, vnto the Prouince of *Patofa*, which were fiftie leagues, is a fat Countrie, beautifull, and very fruitfull, and very well watered, and full of good Riuers. And from thence to the Port *de Spirito Santo*, where wee first ariued in the land of *Florida*, (which may bee 350. leagues, little more or lesse) is a barren land, and the most of it groues of wild Pine-trees, low and full of lakes, and in some places very hie and thicke groues, whither the Indians that were in armes fled, so that no man could find them, neither could any horses enter into them. Which was an inconuenience to the Christians, in regard of the victuals which they found conueied away; and of the trouble which they had in seeking of Indians to bee their guides.

An excellent Countrie for 50. leagues.

CHAP. XIIII.

How the Gouernour departed from the Prouince of Pato-fa, and went through a desert, where he and all his men fell into great distresse, and extreme miserie.

IN the towne of *Patofa* the youth, which the Gouernour carried with him for an interpretour and a guide, began to fome at the mouth, and tumble on the ground, as one possessed with the diuell:

They

They said a Gospell ouer him, and the fit left him. And he said, that foure daies iournie from thence toward the Sunne rising, was the prouince that he spake of. The Indians of *Patofa* said, that toward that part they knew no habitation ; but that toward the Northwest, they knew a Prouince which was called *Coça*, a verie plentifull countrie, which had very great townes in it. The Cacique told the Gouernour, that if he would go thither, he would giue him guides and Indians for burdens; and if he would goe whither the youth spake of, that he would likewise giue him those that he needed : and so with louing words and offers of courtesie, they tooke their leaues the one of the other. Hee gaue him seuen hundred Indians to beare burdens. He tooke Maiz for foure daies iournie. Hee trauelled sixe daies by a path which grew narrow more and more, till it was lost altogether : He went where the youth did

Two swift Riuers.

lead him, and passed two Riuers which were waded : each of them was two crossebowshot ouer : the water came to the stirrops, and had so great a current, that it was needfull for the horsemen to stand one before another, that the footemen might passe aboue them lea-

Another greater Riuer.

ning vnto them. He came to another Riuer of a greater current and largenes, which was passed with more trouble, because the horses did swim at the comming out about a lances length. Hauing passed this Riuer, the Gouernor came to a groue of pinetrees, and threatned the youth, and made as though hee would haue cast him to the dogges, because he had told him a lie,

Nine daies iournie.

saying, it was but foure daies iournie, and they had trauelled nine, and euery day 7. or 8. leagues, and the men by this time were growne wearie and weake, and the horses leane through the great scanting of the

Maiz.

Maiz. The youth said, that hee knew not where hee was. It saued him that he was not cast to the dogges, that there was neuer another whom *Iohn Ortiz* did vnderstand. The Gouernour with them two, and with some horsemen and footemen, leauing the Campe in a groue of pinetrees, trauelled that day 5. or 6. leagues to seek a way, and returned at night very comfortlesse, and without finding any signe of way or towne. The next day there were sundrie opinions deliuered, whether they should goe backe, or what they should doe : and because backward the Countrie whereby they had passed was greatly spoiled and destitute of Maiz, and that which they brought with them was spent, and the men were very weake, and the horses likewise, they doubted much whether they might come to any place where they might helpe themselues. And besides this, they were of opinion, that going in that sort out of order, that any Indians would presume to set vpon them, so that with hunger, or with warre, they could not escape. The Gouernour determined to send horsemen from thence euery way to seeke habitation : and the next day he sent foure Captaines, euery one a sundrie way with eight horsemen. At night they came againe, leading their horses, or driuing them with a sticke before; for they were so wearie, that they could not lead them; neither found they any way nor signe of habitation. The next day, the Gouernour sent other foure with as many horsemen that could swim, to passe the Ose and Riuers which they should find, and they had choice horses the best that were in the Campe. The Captaines were *Baltasar de Gallegos*, which went vp the Riuer; and *Iohn Danusco*, downe the Riuer : *Alfonso Romo*, and *Iohn Rodriguez*

H *Lobillo*

Lobillo went into the inward parts of the land. The
Gouernour brought with him into *Florida* thirteene
sowes, and had by this time three hundred swine: He
commanded euery man should haue halfe a pound of
hogs flesh euery day : and this hee did three or foure
daies, after the Maiz was all spent. With this small
quantitie of flesh, and some sodden hearbs, with much
trouble the people were sustained. The Gouernour
dismissed ý Indians of *Patofa*, because hee had no food
to giue them; who desiring to accompanie and serue
the Christians in their necessitie, making shew that it
grieued them very much to returne, vntill they had left
them in a peopled Countrie, returned to their owne
home. *Iohn Danusco* came on Sunday late in the euening, and brought newes that he had found a little
towne 12. or 13. leagues from thence: he brought a woman and a boy that he tooke there. With his comming
and with those newes, the Gouernour and all the rest
were so glad, that they seemed at that instant to haue
returned from death to life. Vpon Monday, the twentie sixe of Aprill, the Gouernour departed to goe to
the towne, which was called *Aymay*; and the Christians named it the towne of *Reliefe*. He left where the
Camp had lien at the foote of a Pinetree a letter buried, and letters carued in the barke of the pine, the
contents whereof was this: Dig here at the foot of this
pine, & you shal find a letter. And this he did, because
when the Captaines came, which were sent to seeke
some habitation, they might see the letter, and know
what was become of the Gouernour, and which way
he was gone. There was no other way to the town, but
the markes that *Iohn Danusco* left made vpon the trees.
The Gouernour with some of them that had the best
                                                    horses

Margin notes:
The great in-
crease of
swine.

Aymay.

horfes came to it on the Monday : And all the reft in-
forcing themfelues the beft they could, fome of them
lodged within two leagues of the towne, fome within
three and foure, euery one as he was able to goe, and
his ftrength ferued him. There was found in the towne
a ftorehoufe full of the flowre of parched Maiz ; and
fome Maiz, which was diftributed by allowance. Here
were foure Indians taken, and none of them would
confeffe any other thing, but that they knew of none
other habitation. The Gouernour commanded one
of them to be burned ; & prefently another confeffed,
that two daies iournie from thence, there was a Prouince that was called *Cutifa-Chiqui.* Vpon Wednefday
came the Captaines *Baltafar de Gallegos, Alfonfo Romo,*
and *Iohn Rodriguez Lbbillo :* for they had found the letter, and followed the way which the Gouernour had
taken toward the towne. Two men of *Iohn Rodriguez*
companie were loft, becaufe their horfes tired : the
Gouernour checked him very fore for leauing them
behind, and fent to feeke them : and affoone as they
came, he departed toward *Cutifa-Chiqui.* In the way
three Indians were taken, which faid, that the Ladie of
that Countrie had notice alreadie of the Chriftians,
and ftaied for them in a towne of hers. The Gouernour fent by one of them to offer her his friendfhip,
and to aduertife her how hee was comming thither.
The Gouernour came vnto the towne : and prefently
there came foure canoes to him ; in one of them came
a fifter of the Ladie, and approching to the Gouernour
fhe faid thefe words :

*Excellent Lord, my fifter fendeth vnto you by me to kiffe
your Lordfhips hands, and to fignifie vnto you, that the caufe
why fhe came not in perfon, is, that fhe thinketh to do you grea-*

An Indian
burned for his
falfehood.

Cutifa-
chiqui.

ter

ter seruice staying behind, as she doth, giuing order, that with all speed, al her canoes be readie, that your Lordship may passe the Riuer, and take your rest, which shall bee presentlie performed.

The Gouernour gaue her thankes, and she returned to the other side of the Riuer. Within a little while the Ladie came out of the towne in a Chaire, whereon certaine of the principall Indians brought her to the Riuer. She entred into a barge, which had the sterne tilted ouer, and on the floore her mat readie laied with two cushions vpō it one vpon another, where she sate her downe; and with her came her principall Indians in other barges, which did wait vpon her. She went to the place where the Gouernor was, and at her comming she made this speech following:

Excellent Lord, I wish this comming of your Lordship into these your Countries, to be most happie: although my power be not answerable to my wil, and my seruices be not according to my desire, nor such as so high a Prince, as your Lordship, deserueth; yet since the good will is rather to be accepted, then all the treasures of the world, that without it are offered, with most vnfaileable and manifest affection, I offer you my person, lands, and subiects, and this small seruice.

And therewithal she presented vnto him great store of clothes of the Countrie, which shee brought in other canoes; to wit, mantles and skinnes; and tooke from her owne necke a great cordon of perles, and cast it about the necke of the Gouernour, entertaining him with very gracious speeches of loue and courtesie, and commanded canoes to be brought thither, wherein the Gouernour and his people passed the Riuer. Assoone as hee was lodged in the towne, she sent him another present of many hens. This Countrie was verie

A great cordon of perles.

They passe the Riuer. Cutifa-Chiqui.

rie pleasant, fat, and hath goodly meadows by the Riuers. Their woods are thin, and ful of walnut trees and
Mulberrie trees.   They said the sea was two daies iournie from thence.   Within a league, and halfe a league
about this towne, were great townes dispeopled, and
ouergrowne with grasse; which shewed, that they had
been long without inhabitants.   The Indians said, that
two yeere before there was a plague in that Countrie,
and that they remooued to other townes.   There was
in their storehouses great quantitie of clothes, mantles
of yarne made of the barkes of trees, and others made
of feathers, white, greene, red, and yellow, very fine after their vse, and profitable for winter.   There were also many Deeres skinnes, with many compartiments
traced in them, and some of them made into hose,
stockings, and shooes.   And the Ladie perceiuing, that
the Christians esteemed the perles, aduised the Gouernour to send to search certaine graues that were in
that towne, and that hee should find many : and that if
hee would send to the dispeopled townes, hee might
load all his horses.   They sought the graues of that
towne, and there found fourteene rooues of perles,
and little babies and birds made of them.   The people
were browne, well made, and well proportioned, and
more ciuill then any others that were seene in all the
Countrie of *Florida*, and all of them went shod and
clothed.   The youth told the Gouernour, that hee began now to enter into the land which he spake of : and
some credit was giuen him that it was so, because hee
vnderstood the language of the Indians : and hee requested that he might bee Christened, for he said hee
desired to become a Christian :   Hee was Christened,
and named *Peter*; and the Gouernour commanded

him

Walnut trees.
Mulbery trees for silke.
The sea two daies iournie off.

Mantles of the barkes of trees.
Mantles of feathers.

Three hundred ninetie two pounds of pearles found.

him to bee looſed from a chaine, in which vntill that time he had gone. This Countrie, as the Indians reported, had been much inhabited, and had the fame of a good Countrie. And, as it ſeemeth, the youth, which was the Gouernours guide, had heard of it, and that which he knew by hereſay, hee affirmed that hee had ſeene, and augmented at his pleaſure. In this towne was found a dagger, and beades, that had belonged to Chriſtians. The Indians reported, that Chriſtians had been in the hauen, which was two daies iourñie from this towne, many yeeres agoe. Hee that came thither was the Gouernour, the *Licenciate Lucas Vaſquez de Ayllon,* which went to conquer this Countrie, and at his comming to the Port hee died ; and there was a diuiſion, quarrels and ſlaughters betweene ſome principall men which went with him, for the principall gouernment : And without knowing any thing of the Countrie, they returned home to *Hiſpaniola.* All the Companie thought it good to inhabit that Countrie, becauſe it was in a temperat climate : And that if it were inhabited, al the ſhippes of New Spaine, of *Peru, Santa Martha,* and *Tierra firme,* in their returne for *Spaine,* might well touch there : becauſe it was in their way ; and becauſe it was a good Countrie, and ſited fit to raiſe commoditie. The Gouernour, ſince his intent was to ſeeke another treaſure, like that of *Atabalipa* Lord of *Peru,* was not contented with a good Countrie, nor with pearles, though many of them were worth their weight in gold. And if the Countrie had been diuided among the Chriſtians, thoſe which the Indians had fiſhed for afterward, would haue been of more value : for thoſe which they had, becauſe they burned them in the fire, did leeſe their colour. The
Gouernour

This towne was but two daies iournie from the hauen of Santa Helena.

In the yeere 1525.

It is in 32. degrees ½.

Gouernour anſwered them, that vrged him to inhabit, That in all the Countrie, there were not victuals to
ſuſtaine his men one moneth; and that it was needfull
to reſort to the Port of *Ucus,* where *Maldanado* was to
ſtay for them : and that if no richer Countrie were
found, they might returne againe to that whenſoeuer
they would: and in the meane time the Indians would
ſow their fields, and it would be better furniſhed with
Maiz. He inquired of the Indians, whether they had
notice of any great Lord farther into the land. They
told him, that 12. daies iournie from thence, there was
a Prouince called *Chiaha,* ſubiect to the Lord of *Coça.*
Preſently the Gouernour determined to ſeeke that
land. And being a ſterne man, and of few words,
though he was glad to ſift and know the opinion of all
men, yet after hee had deliuered his owne, hee would
not be contraried, and alwaies did what liked himſelfe,
and ſo all men did condeſcend vnto his will. And
though it ſeemed an errour to leaue that Countrie,
(for others might haue been ſought round about,
where the people might haue been ſuſtained, vntill the
harueſt had been readie there, and the Maiz gathered)
yet there was none that would ſay any thing againſt
him, after they knew his reſolution.

Chiaha 12. daies iournie from Santa Helena: and Coſte 7. daies iournie from Chiaha: at which towne of Coſte, they had an oxe hide: Chap. 16.

Chap. XV.

How the Gouernour departed from Cutifa-Chiqui *to ſeeke the Prouince of* Coça ; *and what happened vnto him in the way.*

THe Gouernour departed from *Cutifa-Chiqui*
the third day of May. And becauſe the Indians had reuolted, and the will of the Ladie was
perceiued, that if ſhe could, ſhe would depart without
giuing

giuing any guides or men for burdens, for the wrongs which the Chriſtians had done to the Indians: (for there neuer want ſome among many of a baſe ſort, that for a little gaine doe put themſelues and others in danger of vndoing.) The Gouernour commanded her to be kept in ſafegard, and carried with him, not with ſo good vſage as ſhe deſerued for ẏ good wil ſhe ſhewed, and good entertainement that ſhe had made him. And he verified that old prouerb which ſaith; For weldoing I receiue euill. And ſo he carried her on foot with his bondwomen to looke vnto her. In all the townes where the Gouernour paſſed, the Ladie commanded the Indians to come and carrie the burdens from one towne to another. We paſſed through her Countrie an hundred leagues, in which, as we ſaw, ſhe was much obeyed. For the Indians did all that ſhe commanded them with great efficacie and diligence. *Peter* the youth that was our guide, ſaid, that ſhe was not the Ladie her ſelfe, but a neece of hers, which came to that towne to execute certaine principal men by commandement of the Ladie, which had withheld her tribute: which words were not beleeued, becauſe of the lies which they had found in him before: but they bare with all things, becauſe of the need which they had of him, to declare what the Indians ſaid. In ſeuen daies ſpace the Gouernour came to a Prouince called *Chalaque*, the pooreſt Country of Maiz that was ſeene in *Florida.* The Indians fed vpon rootes and herbes which they ſeeke in the fields, and vpon wild beaſts, which they kil with their bowes and arrowes: and it is a verie gentle people. All of them goe naked, and are very leane. There was a Lord, which for a great preſent, brought the Gouernour two Deeres skins: and there were

Chalaque ſeuen daies iournie from Cutifa-Chiqui.

were in that Countrie many wild hennes. In one 700. Hennes.
towne they made him a prefent of 700. hennes, and fo
in other townes they fent him thofe which they had
or could get. From this Prouince to another, which is
called *Xualla*, he fpent fiue daies : here he found very Xualla 5. daies off.
little Maiz ; and for this caufe, though the people were
wearied, and the horfes very weake, he ftaied no more
but two daies. From *Ocute* to *Cutifa-chiqui*, may bee
fome hundred and thirtie leagues, whereof 80. are
wilderneffe. From *Cutifa-chiqui* to *Xualla*, two hundred
and fiftie, and it is an hillie Countrie. The Gouernour
departed from *Xualla* toward *Guaxule*: he paffed very Rough and hie hilles.
rough and hie hilles. In that iournie, the Ladie of *Cu-*
tifa-chiqui (whom the Gouernour carried with him,
as is afore faid, with purpofe to carrie her to *Guaxule*,
becaufe her territorie reached thither) going on a day
with the bondwomen which lead her, went out of the
way, and entred into a wood, faying, fhe went to eafe
her felfe, and fo fhe deceiued them, and hid her felfe in
the wood ; and though they fought her they could not
find her. She carried away with her a little cheft made
of canes in manner of a coffer, which they call Petaca,
full of vnbored perles. Some which could iudge of
them, faid, that they were of great value. An Indian
woman that waited on her did carrie them. The Gouernour not to difcontent her altogether, left them
with her, making account that in *Guaxule* he would ask
them of her, when he gaue her leaue to returne: which
coffer fhe carried away, and went to *Xualla* with three
flaues which fled from the Campe, and one horfeman
which remained behind, who falling ficke of an ague
went out of the way, and was loft. This man, whofe
name was *Alimamos*, dealt with the flaues to change

I   their

their euill purpose, and returne with him to the Christians: which two of them did; and *Alimamos* and
they ouertooke the Gouernour 50. leagues from
thence in a Prouince called *Chiaha*; and reported how
the Ladie remained in *Xualla* with a slaue of *Andrew
de Vasconcellos*, which would not come backe with
them, and that of a certaintie they liued as man and
wife together, and meant to goe both to *Cutifa-chiqui*.

Within fiue daies the Gouernour came to *Guaxule*.

Guaxule fiue
daies off.

The Indians there gaue him a present of 300. dogges,
because they saw the Christians esteeme them, and
sought them to feed on them: for among them they
are not eaten. In *Guaxule*, and all that way, was very
little Maiz. The Gouernour sent from thence an Indian with a message to the Cacique of *Chiaha*, to desire
him to gather some Maiz thither, that he might rest a
few daies in *Chiaha*. The Gouernour departed from

Canasagua
two daies
iournie off.
Great store of
Mulberrie
trees to make
silke.

Guaxule, and in two daies iournie came to a towne called *Canasagua*. There met him on the way 20. Indians
euery one loaden with a basket ful of Mulberries: for
there be many, and those very good, from *Cutifa-chiqui*
thither, and so forward in other Prouinces, and also
nuts and plummes. And the trees grow in the fields
without planting or dressing them, and are as big and
as rancke, as though they grew in gardens digged and
watered. From the time that the Gouernour departed from *Canasagua*, hee iournied fiue daies through a
desert; and two leagues before hee came to *Chiaha*,
there met him 15. Indians loaden with Maiz, which
the Cacique had sent; and they told him on his behalfe, that he waited his comming with 20. barnes full
of it; and farther, that himselfe, his Countrie, and subiects, & al things els were at his seruice. On the 5. day of
Iune

Iune, the Gouernor entred into *Chiaha*: The Cacique voided his owne houses, in which he lodged, & receiued him with much ioy, saying these words following:

Mightie and excellent Lord, I hold my selfe for so happie a man, in that it hath pleased your Lordship to vse me, that nothing could haue happened vnto me of more contentment, nor that I would haue esteemed so much. From Guaxule *your Lordship sent vnto me, that I should prepare Maiz for you in this towne for two moneths: Here I haue for you 20. barnes full of the choisest that in all the Countrie could be found. If your Lordship bee not entertained by me in such sort, as is fit for so hie a Prince, respect my tender age, which excuseth me from blame, and receiue my good wil, which with much loyaltie, truth, and sinceritie, I will alwaies shew in any thing, which shall conserue your Lordships seruice.*

The Gouernor answered him, that he thanked him very much for his seruice and offer, and that he would alwaies account him as his brother. There was in this towne much butter in gourds melted like oile: they said it was the fat of beares. There was found also great store of oile of walnuts, which was cleare as butter, and of a good taste, and a pot full of honie of bees, which neither before nor afterward was seene in all the Countrie. The towne was in an Island betweene two armes of a Riuer, and was seated nigh one of them. The Riuer diuideth it selfe into those two branches two crossebow shot aboue the towne, and meeteth againe a league beneath the same. The plaine betweene both the branches is sometimes one crossebow shot, sometimes two crossebow shot ouer. The branches are very broad, and both of them may be waded ouer. There were all along them verie good meadows, and manie fields sowne with Maiz. And

The fat of beares.
Oile of Walnuts.
Honie of Bees.
Chiaha seated in an Island.

because

because the Indians staied in their towne, the Gouernour only lodged in the houses of the Cacique, and his people in the fields; where there was euer a tree, euerie one tooke one for himselfe. Thus the Camp lay separated one from another, and out of order. The Gouernour winked at it, because the Indians were in peace, and because it was very hot, and the people should haue suffered great extremitie, if it had not bin so. The horses came thither so weake, that for feeblenesse, they were not able to carrie their masters: because that from *Cutifa-chiqui,* they alwaies trauelled with verie little prouender, and were hunger-starued and tired euer since they came from the desert of *Ocute.* And because the most of them were not in case to vse in battell, though need should require, they sent them to feed in the night a quarter of a league from the Camp.

The desert of Ocute, chap. 14.

The Christians were there in great danger, because that if at this time the Indians had set vpon them, they had been in euill case to haue defended themselues. The Gouernour rested there thirtie daies, in which time, because the Countrie was very fruitfull, the horses grew fat. At the time of his departure, by the importunitie of some, which would haue more then was reason, hee demanded of the Cacique 30. women to make slaues of. Hee answered that he would conferre with his chiefe men. And before hee returned an answere, one night all of them with their wiues and children forsooke the towne, and fled away. The next day the Gouernour purposing to goe to seeke them, the Cacique came vnto him, and at his comming vsed these words vnto the Gouernour:

30. Daies rest.

Mightie Lord, with shame and feare of your Lordship, because my subiects against my will haue done amisse in ab-

senting

senting themselues, I went my way without your licenfe ; and knowing the errour which I haue committed, like a loyall fubiect, I come to yeeld my felfe into your power, to dispose of mee at your owne pleafure. For my fubiects do not obey mee, nor doe any thing but what an Vncle of mine commandeth, which gouerneth this Countrie for me, vntill I be of a perfect age. If your Lordfhip will purfue them, and execute on them that, which for their difobedience they deferue, I will be your guide, fince at this prefent my fortune will not fuffer me to performe any more.

Prefently the Gouernour with 30. horfemen, and as many footemen, went to feeke the Indians; and paffing by fome townes of the principall Indians which had abfented themfelues, hee cut and deftroyed great fields of Maiz ; and went vp the Riuer, where the Indians were in an Ifland, where the horfemen could not come at them. There he fent them word by an Indian to returne to their towne and feare nothing, and that they fhould giue him men to carrie burdens, as af thofe behind had done ; for he would haue no Indian women, feeing they were fo loth to part with them. The Indians accepted his requeft, and came to the Gouernour to excufe themfelues; and fo all of them returned to their towne. A Cacique of a Prouince caleld *Cofte*, came to this towne to vifit the Gouernour. After hee had offered himfelfe, and paffed with him fome words of tendring his feruice and curtefie; the Gouernour asking him whether he had notice of any rich Countrie ? he faid, yea : to wit, that toward the North, there was a Prouince named *Chifca* : and that there was a melting of copper, and of another metall of the fame colour, faue that it was finer, and of a farre more perfect colour, and farre better to the fight ; and

Certaine townes.

Mines of copper and gold in Chifca toward the North.

that

I 3

"that they vsed it not so much, because it was softer. And the selfe same thing was told the Gouernour in *Cutifa-chiqui*; where we saw some little hatchets of copper, which were said to haue a mixture of gold. But in that part the Countrie was not well peopled, and they said there were mountaines, which the horses could not passe: and for that cause, the Gouernour would not goe from *Cutifa-chiqui* directly thither: And hee made account, that trauelling through a peopled Countrie, when his men and horses should bee in better plight, and hee were better certified of the truth of the thing, he would returne toward it, by mountaines, and a better inhabited Countrie, whereby hee might haue better passage. He sent two Christians from *Chiaha* with certaine Indians which knew the Countrie of *Chisca*, and the language thereof to view it, and to make report of that which they should find; where he told them that he would tarrie for them.

Hatchets of copper holding gold.

Chisca is directly North from Cutifa-Chiqui, which is within two daies of Santa Helena.

Two Christians sent from Chiaha to seeke Chisca.

Chap. XVI.

How the Gouernor departed from Chiaha, and at Coste was in danger to haue beene slaine by the hands of the Indians, and by a stratageme escaped the same: And what more happened vnto him in this iournie, and how he came to Coça.

Hen the Gouernour was determined to depart from *Chiaha to Coste*, he sent for the Cacique to come before him, and with gentle words tooke his leaue of him, and gaue him certaine things, wherewith he rested much contented: In seuen daies hee came to *Coste*. The second of Iulie he commanded his Campe to be pitched

Coste seuen daies from Chiaha, chap. 14.

ed

ed two croſſebow ſhot from the town: and with eight
men of his guard he went where he found the Cacique, which to his thinking receiued him with great
loue. As heé was talking with him, there went from
the Campe certaine footemen to the towne to ſeeke
ſome Maiz, and not contented with it, they ranſacked
and ſearched the houſes, and tooke what they found.
With this deſpite the Indians began to riſe and to take
their armes: and ſome of them with cudgils in their
hands, ran vpon fiue or ſixe Chriſtians, which had
done them wrong, and beat them at their pleaſure.
The Gouernour ſeeing them al in an vprore, and himſelfe among them with ſo few Chriſtians, to eſcape
their hands vſed a ſtratagem, farre againſt his owne diſ- A wiſe ſtra-
poſition, being, as hee was, very francke and open: and tagem.
though it grieued him very much that any Indian
ſhould be ſo bold, as with reaſon, or without reaſon to
deſpiſe the Chriſtians, he tooke vp a cudgel, and tooke
their parts againſt his owne men; which was a meanes
to quiet them: And preſently he ſent word by a man
very ſecretly to the Campe, that ſome armed men
ſhould come toward the place where he was; and hee
tooke the Cacique by the hand, vſing very mild words
vnto him, and with ſome principall Indians that did
accompanie him, he drew them out of the towne into
a plaine way, and vnto the ſight of the Campe, whither by little and little with good diſcretion the Chriſtians began to come and to gather about them. Thus
the Gouernour led the Cacique, and his chiefe men
vntill he entred with them into the Campe: and neere
vnto his tent, bee commanded them to be put in ſafe
cuſtodie; and told them, that they ſhould not depart
without giuing him a guide and Indians for burthens,
and

and till certaine sicke Christians were come, which he had commanded to come downe the Riuer in canoes from *Chiaha*; and those also which he had sent to the Prouince of *Chisca*: (for they were not returned; and he feared that the Indians had slaine the one, and the other.) Within three daies after, those which were sent to *Chisca* returned, and made report, that the Indians had carried them through a Countrie so poore of Maiz, and so rough, and ouer so high mountaines, that it was impossible for the armie to trauell that way; and that seeing the way grew very long, and that they lingred much, they consulted to returne from a little poore towne, where they saw nothing that was of any profit, and brought an oxe hide, which the Indians gaue them, as thinne as a calues skinne, and the haire like a soft wooll, betweene the course and fine wooll of sheepe. The Cacique gaue a guide, and men for burdens, and departed with the Gouernours leaue. The Gouernour departed from *Coste* the ninth of Iulie, and lodged at a towne called *Tali*: The Cacique came foorth to receiue him on the way, and made this speech:

Excellent Lord and Prince, worthie to be serued and obeyed of all the Princes in the world; howsoeuer for the most part by the outward physiognomie, the inward vertue may bee iudged, and that who you are, and of what strength, was knowne vnto mee before now: I will not inferre hereupon how meane I am in your presence, to hope that my poore seruices will bee gratefull and acceptable: since whereas strength faileth, the will doth not cease to be praised and accepted. And for this cause I presume to request your Lordship, that you will be pleased onely to respect the same, and consider wherein you will command my seruice in this your Countrie.

The

Those which were sent to seeke Chisca returne.
High mountaines.

A little poore towne.
An oxe hide with haire like wooll. cap. 16. and Gomara Histor. Generall. cap. 215. saith so.
Tali, 1 day from Coste.

The Gouernour answered him, that his good will and offer was as acceptable vnto him, as if he had offered him all the treasures of the world; and that hee would alwaies intreate, fauour, and esteeme him as if he were his owne brother. The Cacique commanded prouision necessarie for two daies, while the Gouernour was there, to be brought thither: and at the time of his departure, he gaue him foure women and two men, which hee had need of to beare burthens. The Gouernour trauelled sixe daies through many townes subiect to the Cacique of *Coça*: & as he entred into his Countrie many Indians came vnto him euery day from the Cacique, and met him on the way with messages, one going, and another comming. Hee came to *Coça* vpon Friday, the 26. of Iulie. The Cacique came foorth to receiue him two crossebow shot from the towne in a chaire, which his principall men carried on their shoulders, sitting vpon a cushion, and couered with a garment of Marterns, of the fashion and bignes of a womans huke: hee had on his head a diadem of feathers, and round about him many Indians playing vpon flutes, and singing. Assoone as he came vnto the Gouernour, he did his obeysance, and vttered these words following:

Excellent and mightie Lord, aboue all them of the earth; although I come but now to receiue you, yet I haue receiued you many daies agoe in my heart, to wit, from the day wherein I had first notice of your Lordship; with so great desire to serue you, with so great pleasure and contentment, that this which I make shew of, is nothing in regard of that which is in my heart, neither can it haue any kind of comparison. This you may hold for certaine, that to obtaine the dominion of the whole world, would not haue re-

K *ioyced*

Many townes of Coça.

Coça. Iulie 26.

Marterns.

ioyced me so much, as your sight, neither would I haue held it for so great a felicitie. Doe not looke for me to offer you that which is your owne: to wit, my person, my lands and subiects: onely I will busie my selfe in commanding my men with all diligence and due reuerence to welcome you from hence to the towne with playing and singing, where your Lordship shall be lodged and attended vpon by my selfe and them: and all that I possesse, your Lordship shall vse as it were your owne. For your Lordship shall doe me a verie great fauour in so doing.

The Gouernour gaue him thankes, and with great ioy they both went conferring together, till they came to the towne: and he commanded his Indians to void their houses, wherein the Gouernor and his men were lodged. There was in the barnes, and in the fields, great store of Maiz and French Beanes: The Country was greatly inhabited with many great townes, and many sowne fields, which reached from the one to the other. It was pleasant, fat, full of good meadows vpon Riuers. There were in the fields, many Plum trees, aswell of such as grow in *Spaine*, as of the Countrie: and wild tall vines, that runne vp the trees; and besides these, there were other low vines with big and sweet grapes; but for want of digging and dressing, they had great kirnels in them. The Gouernour vsed to set a guard ouer the Caciques, because they should not absent themselues, and carried them with him, till he came out of their Countries: because that carrying them along with him, he looked to find people in the townes, and they gaue him guides, and men to carrie burdens: and before hee went out of their Countries, he gaue them licence to returne to their houses, and to their porters likewise, assoone as he came to any other Lordship, where they gaue him others. The men of

[margin: The towne.]

[margin: Many great townes.]

[margin: Many plumtrees of diuers sorts. Two sorts of grapes.]

of *Coça* seeing their Lord detained, tooke it in euil part, and reuolted, and hid themselues in the woods, alwell those of the towne of the Cacique, as those of the other townes of his principall subiects. The Gouernor sent out foure Captaines, euery one his way to seeke them. They tooke many men and women, which were put into chaines: They seeing the hurt which they receiued, and how little they gained in absenting themselues, came againe, promising to do whatsoeuer they were commanded. Of those which were taken prisoners, some principall men were set at libertie, whom the Cacique demanded: and euery one that had any, carried the rest in chaines like slaues, without letting them goe to their Countrie: neither did any returne, but some few, whose fortune helped them with the good diligence which they vsed to file off their chaines by night, or such as in their trauelling could slippe aside out of the way, seeing any negligence in them that kept them: some escaped away with the chaines, and with the burdens, and clothes which they carried.

Chap. XVII.
How the Gouernour went from Coça *to* Tascaluca.

He Gouernour rested in *Coça* 25.daies. He departed from thence the 20. of August to seeke a Prouince called *Tascaluca*: hee carried with him the Cacique of *Coça*. He passed that day by a great towne called *Tallimuchase*, the people were fled: he lodged halfe a league farther neere a brooke. The next day he came to a towne called *Ytaua*, subiect to *Coça*. Hee staied there

20. of August.

Tallimuchase, a great towne.

Ytaua.

there sixe daies because of a Riuer that passed by it,
which at that time was very hie; and assoone as the Riuer suffered him to passe, he set forward, and lodged at
a towne named *Vllibahali*. There came to him on the
way, on the Caciques behalfe of that Prouince, ten or
twelue principall Indians to offer him his seruice; all
of them had their plumes of feathers, and bowes and
arrowes. The Gouernour comming to the towne
with twelue horsemen, and some footemen of his
guard, leauing his people a crossebow shot from the
towne, entred into it, hee found all the Indians with
their weapons: and as farre as he could ghesse, they seemed to haue some euill meaning. It was knowne afterward, that they were determined to take the Cacique of *Coça* from the Gouernour, if hee had requested
it. The Gouernour commanded all his people to enter the towne, which was walled about, and neere vnto it passed a small Riuer. The wall, aswell of that, as of
others, which afterward wee saw, was of great posts
thrust deepe into the ground and very rough, and many long railes as big as ones arme laid acrosse between
them, and the wall was about the height of a lance, and
it was daubed within and without with clay, and had
loope holes. On the otherside of the Riuer was a
towne, where at that present the Cacique was. The
Gouernour sent to call him, and hee came presently.
After he had passed with the Gouernour some words
of offering his seruices, he gaue him such men for his
cariages as he needed, and thirtie women for slaues. In
that place was a Christian lost, called *Mançano*, borne
in *Salamanca*, of noble parentage, which went astray to
seeke for grapes, whereof there is great store, and those
very good. The day that the Gouernour departed
from

from thence, he lodged at a towne subiect to the Lord ^{A towne.} of *Vllibabali*: and the next day hee came to another towne called *Toasi*. The Indians gaue the Gouernour ^{Toasi.} thirtie women, and such men for his cariages as he needed. Hee trauelled ordinarily 5. or 6. leagues a day ^{He trauelled} when he trauelled through peopled Countries: and ^{ordinarily fiue or sixe leagues} going through deserts, he marched as fast as he could, ^{a day.} to eschew the want of Maiz. From *Toasi*, passing through some townes subiect to a Cacique, which was Lord of a prouince called *Tallise*, hee trauelled fiue daies: He came to *Tallise* the 18. of September: The towne was great, and situated neere vnto a maine Ri-^{Tallise, a great} uer. On the other side of the Riuer were other townes, ^{towne.}^{September 18.} and many fields sowne with Maiz. On both sides it ^{A maine Ri-} was a very plentifull Countrie, and had store of Maiz: ^{uer.} they had voided the towne. The Gouernour commanded to call the Cacique; who came, and betweene them passed some words of loue and offer of his seruices, and hee presented vnto him 40. Indians. There came to the Gouernour in this towne a principall Indian in the behalfe of the Cacique of *Tascaluca*, and made this speech following:

Mightie, vertuous, and esteemed Lord, the great Cacique of Tascaluca *my Lord, sendeth by me to kisse your Lordships hands, and to let you vnderstand, that he hath notice, how you iustly rauish with your perfections and power, all men on the earth; and that euerie one by whom your Lordship passeth doth serue and obey you; which he acknowledgeth to be due vnto you, and desireth, as his life, to see, and to serue your Lordship. For which cause by me he offereth himselfe, his lands and subiects, that when your Lordship pleaseth to go through his Countrie, you may be receiued with all peace and loue, serued and obeyed; and that in recompense of the desire*

he

*he hath to see you, you will doe him the fauour to let him know
when you will come : for how much the sooner, so much the
greater fauour he shall receiue.*

The Gouernour receiued and dispatched him gra-
ciously, giuing him beades, which among them were
not much esteemed, and some other things to carrie to
his Lord. And he gaue licence to the Cacique of *Coça*
to returne home to his owne Countries. The Cacique
of *Tallise* gaue him such men for burthens as he needed. And after he had rested there 20. daies, hee departed thence toward *Tascaluca*. That day when hee
went from *Tallise*, hee lodged at a great towne called

*Casiste a great
towne.
Tascaluca.*

Casiste. And the next day passed by another, and came
to a small towne of *Tascaluca*; and the next day hee
camped in a wood two leagues from the towne where
the Cacique resided, and was at that time. And he sent
the Master of the Camp, *Luys de Moscoso*, with 15.
horsemen, to let him know how hee was comming.
The Cacique was in his lodgings vnder a Canopie:
and without doores, right against his lodgings, in an
high place, they spread a mat for him, & two cushions
one vpon another, where he sat him downe, and his Indians placed themselues round about him, somewhat
distant from him, so that they made a place, and a void
roome where he sate : and his chiefest men were neerest to him, and one with a shadow of Deeres skinne,
which keept the Sunne from him, being round, and of
the bignes of a target, quartered with black and white,
hauing a rundell in the middest : a farre off it seemed
to be of taffata, because ỹ colours were very perfect. It
was set on a small staffe stretched wide out. This was
the deuice which hee carried in his warres. Hee was a
man of a very tall stature, of great limmes, and spare,
and

and well proportioned, and was much feared of his neighbours and subiects. He was Lord of many territories and much people : In his countenance hee was very graue. After the Master of the Campe had spoken with him, he and those that went with him coursed their horses, pransing them to and fro, and now and then toward the place where the Cacique was, who with much grauitie and dissimulation now and then lifted vp his cies, and beheld them as it were with disdaine. At the Gouernours comming, hee made no offer at all to rise. The Gouernour tooke him by the hand, and both of them sat downe together on a seate which was vnder the cloth of estate. The Cacique said these words vnto him :

Mighty Lord, I bid your Lordship right hartily welcome. I receiue as much pleasure and contentment with your sight, as if you were my brother whom I dearely loued : vpon this point it is not needfull to vse many reasons : since it is no discretion to speake that in many wordes, which in few may be vttered. How much the greater the will is, so much more giueth it name to the workes, and the workes giue testimonie of the truth. Now touching my will, by it you shall know, how certain & manifest it is, and how pure inclination I haue to serue you. Concerning the fauour which you did me, in the things which you sent me, I make as much account of them as is reason to esteeme them : and chiefly because they were yours. Now see what seruice you will command me.

The Gouernor satisfied him with sweet words, and with great breuitie. When hee departed from thence he determined to carrie him along with him for some causes, and at two daies iournie hee came to a towne called *Piache*, by which there passed a great Riuer. The Gouernour demanded canoes of the Indians : they said,

Piache.
A great Riuer.

said, they had them not, but that they would make
rafts of canes and drie timber, on which he might passe
well enough: And they made them with all diligence
and speed, and they gouerned them; and because the
water went very slow, the Gouernour and his people
passed very well.

From the Port *de Spirito Santo* to *Apalache,* which
is about an hundred leagues, the Gouernour went
from East to West: And from *Apalache* to *Cutifa-chiqui,* which are 430. leagues, from the Southwest to the
Northeast: and from *Cutifa-chiqui* to *Xualla,* which are
about two hundred and fiftie leagues, from the South
to the North: And from *Xualla* to *Tascaluca,* which are
two hundred and fiftie leagues more, an hundred and
ninetie of them he trauelled from East to West, to wit,
to the Prouince of *Coça:* and the other 60. from *Coça*
to *Tascaluca* from the North to the South.

Hauing passed the Riuer of *Piache,* a Christian went
from his companie from thence to seeke a woman
slaue that was runne away from him, and the Indians
either tooke him captiue, or slue him. The Gouernor vrged the Cacique that he should giue account of
him, and threatned him, that if he were not found, he
would neuer let him loose. The Cacique sent an Indian from thence to *Mauilla,* whither they were trauelling, which was a towne of a principall Indian and
his subiect, saying, that he sent him to aduise them to
make readie victuals, and men for carriages. But, (as
afterward appeared) hee sent him to assemble all the
men of warre thither, that hee had in his Countrie.
The Gouernour trauelled three daies; and the third

Mauilla.
13. Of Octo-
ber. day he passed all day through a peopled Countrie: and
he came to *Mauilla* vpon Monday the 18. of October

ber. He went before the Camp with 15. horsemen
and 30. footemen. And from the towne came a Chriftian, whom he had fent to the principall man, three or
foure daies before, becaufe he fhould not abfent himfelfe, and alfo to learne in what fort the Indians were:
who told him that hee thought they were in an euill
purpofe: for while hee was there, there came manie people into the towne, and many weapons, and
that they made great hafte to fortifie the wall. *Luys* Mauilla
de *Mofcofo* told the Gouernour, that it would bee walled.
good to lodge in the field, feeing the Indians were
of fuch difpofition: and hee anfwered, that he would
lodge in the towne, for hee was wearie of lodging
in the field. When hee came neere vnto the towne,
the Cafique came foorth to receiue him with many
Indians playing vpon flutes and finging: And after
hee had offered himfelfe, hee prefented him with
three mantles of marterns. The Gouernour, with 3. Mantles of
both the Caciques, and feuen or eight men of his Marterns.
guard, and three or foure horfemen, which alighted
to accompanie him, entred into the towne, and fat
him downe vnder a cloth of eftate. The Cacique
of *Tafcaluca* requefted him, that hee would let him remaine in that towne, and trouble him no more with
trauelling: And feeing he would not giue him leaue,
in his talke he changed his purpofe, and diffemblinglie
fained that he would fpeake with fome principall Indians, and rofe vp from the place where hee fate with
the Gouernour, and entred into a houfe, where many
Indians were with their bowes and arrowes. The Gouernour when he faw he returned not, called him, and
he anfwered, that he would not come out from thence,

L   neither

neither would he goe any farther then that towne, and
that if he would goe his way in peace, hee should prefently depart, and should not feeke to carrie him perforce out of his Countrie and territorie.

Chap. XVIII.

*How the Indians rofe againft the Gouernour, and what
enfued thereupon.*

He Gouernour feeing the determination, and furious anfwere of the
Cacique, went about to pacifie
him with faire words : to which he
gaue no anfwere, but rather with
much pride and difdaine, withdrew himfelfe where the Gouernor
might not fee him, nor fpeake with him. As a principall Indian paffed that way, the Gouernor called him,
to fend him word, that hee might remaine at his pleafure in his Countrie, and that it would pleafe him to
giue him a guide, and men for carriages, to fee if hee
could pacifie him with mild words. The Indians anfwered with great pride, that hee would not hearken
vnto him. *Baltafar de Gallegos,* which ftood by, tooke
hold of a gowne of marterns which hee had on ; and
hee caft it ouer his head, and left it in his hands : and
becaufe all of them immediatly began to ftirre, *Baltafar de Gallegos* gaue him fuch a wound with his cou-
tilas, that hee opened him downe the backe, and
prefently all the Indians with a great crie came out
of the houfes fhooting their arrowes. The Gouernour confideing, that if hee tarried there, hee could
not efcape, and if hee commanded his men to come

*A gowne of
marterns.*

in,

in, which were without the towne, the Indians within the houſes might kill their horſes, and doe much
hurt, ranne out of the towne, and beforehee came
out, hee fell twice or thrice, and thoſe that were
with him did helpe him vp againe; and he and thoſe
that were with him were ſore wounded: and in a mo-
ment there were fiue Chriſtians ſlaine in the towne.
The Gouernour came running out of the towne, crying out, that euery man ſhould ſtand farther off, becauſe from the wall they did them much hurt. The Indians ſeeing that the Chriſtians retired, and ſome of
them, or the moſt part, more then an ordinary paſe, ſhot
with great boldneſſe at them, and ſtrooke downe ſuch
as they could ouertake. The Indians which the Chriſtians did lead with them in chaines, had laid downe
their burthens neere vnto the wall: and aſſoone as the
Gouernour and his men were retired, the men of *Mauilla* laid them on the Indians backs againe, and tooke
them into the towne, and looſed them preſently from
their chaines, and gaue them bowes and arrowes to
fight withall. Thus they poſſeſſed themſelues of al the
clothes and perles, and all that the Chriſtians had,
which their ſlaues carried. And becauſe the Indians
had been alwaies peaceable vntill wee came to this
place, ſome of our men had their weapons in their far-
dels and remained vnarmed. And from others that
had entred the towne with the Gouernour they had
taken ſwords and halebards, and fought with them.
When the Gouernour was gotten into the field, hee
called for an horſe, and with ſome that accompanied
him, hee returned and ſlew two or three Indians: All
the reſt retired themſelues to the towne, and ſhot with
their bowes from the wall. And thoſe which preſu-

*Al the clothes
and perles of
the Chriſtians
were loſt.*

med of their nimblenes, fallied foorth to fight a ftones
caft from the wall: And when the Chriftians charged them, they retired themfelues at their leafure
into the towne. At the time that the broile began,
there were in the towne a Frier, and a Prieft, and
a feruant of the Gouernour, with a woman flaue: and
they had no time to come out of the towne: and they
tooke an houfe, and fo remained in the towne. The
Indians being become Mafters of the place, they fhut
the doore with a field gate: and among them was one
fword which the Gouernours feruant had, and with it
he fet himfelfe behind the doore, thrufting at the Indians which fought to come into them: and the Frier
and the Prieft ftood on the other fide, each of them
with a barre in their hands to beate him downe that
firft came in. The Indians feeing they could not get
in by the doore, began to vncouer the houfe top. By
this time, all the horfemen and footemen which were
behind, were come to *Mauilla*. Here there were fun-
drie opinions, whether they fhould charge the Indians
to enter the towne, or whether they fhould leaue it,
becaufe it was hard to enter: and in the end it was refolued to fet vpon them.

Chap. XIX.
*How the Gouernour fet his men in order, and entred the
towne of* Mauilla.

Ssoone as the battell and the rereward were
come to *Mauilla*, the Gouernour commanded all thofe that were beft armed to
alight, and made foure fquadrons of footmen. The Indians, feeing how he was fetting his men
in

in order, concluded with the Cacique, that hee should goe his way, saying vnto him, as after it was knowne by certaine women that were taken there, that he was but one man, and could fight but for one man, and that they had there among them many principall Indians verie valiant and expert in feates of armes, that any one of them was able to order the people there; and forasmuch as matters of warre were subiect to casualtie, and it was vncertaine which part should ouercome, they wished him to saue himselfe, to the end, that if it fel out that they should end their daies there, as they determined, rather then to be ouercome, there might remaine one to gouerne the Countrie. For all this hee would not haue gon away: but they vrged him so much, that with fifteene or twentie Indians of his owne, hee went out of the towne, and carried away a skarlat cloke, and other things of the Christians goods; as much as hee was able to carrie, and seemed best vnto him. The Gouernour was informed how there went men out of the towne, and hee commanded the horsemen to beset it, and sent in euery squadron of footemen one souldier with a firebrand to set fire on the houses, that the Indians might haue no defense: all his men being set in order, hee commanded an harcubuz to bee shot off. The signe being giuen, the foure squadrons, euery one by it selfe with great furie, gaue the onset; and with great hurt on both sides they entred the towne. The Prier and the Priest, and those that were with them in the house were saued, which cost the liues of two men of account, and valiant, which came thither to succour them. The Indians fought with such courage, that many times they draue our men out of the towne. The fight lasted so long, that for wearinesse and great thirst

many

many of the Christians went to a poole that was neere the wal, to drink, which was all stained with the blood of the dead, and then came againe to fight. The Gouernour seeing this, entred among the footemen into the towne on horseback, with certaine that accompanied him, and was a meane that the Christians came to set fire on the houses, and brake and ouercame the Indians, who running out of the towne from the footemen, the horsemen without draue in at the gates again, where being without all hope of life, they fought valiantly, & after the Christians came among the to handy blowes, seeing themselues in great distresse without any succour, many of them fled into the burning houses, where one vpon another they were smothered **The death of** and burnt in the fire. The whole number of the Indi-**2500. Indians.** ans that died in this towne, were two thousand and fiue hundred, little more or lesse. Of the Christians there died eighteene; of which one was *Don Carlos*, brother in law to the Gouernour, and a nephew of his, and one *Iohn de Gamez*, and *Men Rodriguez* Portugals, and *Iohn Vazquez de Villanoua de Barca Rota*, all men of honour, and of much valour: the rest were footemen. Besides those that were slaine, there were an hundred and fiftie wounded with 700. wounds of their arrowes: and it pleased God that of very dangerous wounds they were quickly healed. Moreouer, there were twelue horses slaine, and seuentie hurt. All the clothes which the Christians carried with them to clothe themselues withall, and the ornaments to say Masse, and the perles, were all burnt there: and the Christians did set them on fire themselues; because they held for a greater inconuenience, the hurt which the Indians might doe them from those houses, where
they

they had gathered all those goods together, then the losse of them. Here the Gouernour vnderstood, that *Francisco Maldonado* waited for him at the Port of *Ochuse*, and that it was sixe daies iournie from thence; and he dealt with *Iohn Ortiz* to keepe it secret, because he had not accomplished that which he determined to doe; and because the perles were burnt there, which he meant to haue sent to *Cuba* for a shew, that the people hearing the newes, might be desirous to come to that Countrie. He feared also, that if they should haue newes of him without seeing from *Florida* neither gold nor siluer, nor any thing of value, it would get such a name, that no man would seeke to goe thither, when he should haue neede of people. And so he determined to send no newes of himselfe, vntill hee had found some rich Countrie.

The Port of Ochuse sixe daies iournie from Mauilla.

Chap. XX.
How the Gouernour departed from Mauilla *toward* Chicaça, *and what happened vnto him.*

FRom the time that the Gouernour entred into *Florida*, vntill his departure from *Mauilla*, there died an hundred and two Christians, some of sicknesse, and others which the Indians slew. He staied in *Mauilla*, because of the wounded men, eight and twentie daies; all which time he lay in the field. It was a well inhabited and a fat Countrie, there were some great & walled townes: and many houses scattered all about the fields, to wit, a crossebow shot or two, the one from the other. Vpon Sonday, the eighteenth of Nouember, when the hurt men were knowne to bee healed, the Gouernour departed

Great and walled townes

18. Of Nouember.

departed from *Mauilla*. Euery one furnished himselfe with Maiz for two daies, and they trauelled fiue
daies through a desert : they came to a Prouince called

Taliepataua.
Pasallaya, vnto a towne, named *Taliepataua* : and from

Cabusto.
thence they went to another, called *Cabusto* : neere vn-

A great Riuer.
to it ran a great Riuer. The Indians on the other side
cried out, threatning the Christians to kill them, if they
sought to passe it. The Gouernour commanded his
men to make a barge within the towne, because the Indians should not perceiue it : it was finished in foure
daies, and being ended, he commanded it to be carried
one night vpon sleds halfe a league vp the Riuer. In
the morning there entred into it thirtie men well armed. The Indians perceiued what was attempted,
and those which were neerest, came to defend the passage. They resisted what they could, till the Christians came neere them ; and seeing that the barge came

Canauarales.
to the shore, they fled away into the groues of canes.
The Christians mounted on horsebacke, and went vp
the Riuer to make good the passage, whereby the Gouernour and his companie passed the Riuer. There

Some townes.
were along the Riuer some townes well stored with
Maiz and French Beanes. From thence to *Chicaça* the
Gouernour trauelled fiue daies through a desert. Hee

A Riuer.
came to a Riuer, where on the otherside were Indians
to defend the passage. He made another barge in two
daies ; and when it was finished, the Gouernour sent
an Indian to request the Cacique to accept of his
friendship, and peaceably to expect his comming :
whom the Indians that were on the other side the Riuer slew before his face, and presently making a great
shout went their way. Hauing passed the Riuer, the

December 17.
next day, being the 17. of December, the Gouernour
came

came to *Chicaça*, a small towne of twentie houses. And
after they were come to *Chicaça*, they were much trou- Chicaça.
bled with cold, because it was now winter and it snow- Snow and
ed, while most of them were lodged in the field, be- much cold.
fore they had time to make themselues houses. This
Countrie was very well peopled, and the houses scattered like those of *Mauilla*, fat and plentifull of Maiz,
and the most part of it was fielding: they gathered
as much as sufficed to passe the winter. Some Indians
were taken, among which was one whom the Cacique esteemed greatly. The Gouernour sent an Indian to signifie to the Cacique, that he desired to see him
and to haue his friendship. The Cacique came vnto
him, to offer him his person, Countrie and subiects,
and told him, that he would cause two other Caciques
to come to him in peace; who within few daies after
came with him, and with their Indians: The one was
called *Alimamu*, the other *Nicalasa*. They gaue a present vnto the Gouernour of an hundred and fiftie co- Conies.
nies, and of the Countrie garments, to wit, of mantles
and skinnes. The Cacique of *Chicaça* came to visit
him many times; and sometimes the Gouernour sent
to call him, and sent him an horse to goe and come. He
complained vnto him, that a subiect of his was risen a-
gainst him and depriued him of his tribute, requesting
his aide against him, for hee meant to seeke him in his
Countrie, and to punish him according to his desert. An Indian
Which was nothing els but a fained plot. For they de- stratageme.
termined, assoone as the Gouernour was gone with
him, and the Campe was diuided into two parts, the
one part of them to set vpon the Gouernour, and the
other vpon them that remained in *Chicaça*. Hee went
to the towne where he vsed to keepe his residence, and
M   brought

brought with him two hundred Indians with their bowes and arrowes. The Gouernour tooke thirtie horſemen, and eightie footemen, and they went to *Saquechuma* (for ſo was the Prouince called of that chiefe man, which he ſaid had rebelled.) They found a walled towne, without any men : and thoſe which went with the Cacique ſet fire on the houſes, to diſſemble their treaſon. But by reaſon of the great care and heedfulneſſe, that was as well in the Gouernours people which hee carried with him, as of thoſe which remained in *Chicaça*, they durſt not aſſault them at that time. The Gouernour inuited the Cacique, and certaine principall Indians, and gaue them hogges fleſh to eate. And though they did not commonly vſe it, yet they were ſo greedie of it, that euery night there came Indians to certaine houſes a croſſebow ſhot from the Camp, where the hogges lay, and killed, and carried away as many as they could. And three Indians were taken in the manner. Two of them the Gouernor commanded to be ſhot to death with arrowes ; & to cut off the hands of the other ; & he ſent him ſo handled to the Cacique. Who made as though it grieued him ỹ they had offended the Gouernor, and that he was glad that he had executed that puniſhment on them. He lay in a plaine Countrie halfe a league from the place, where the Chriſtians lodged. Foure horſemen went a ſtragling thither, to wit, *Franciſco Oſorio*, and a ſeruant of the Marques of *Aſtorga*, called *Reynoſo*, and two ſeruants of the Gouernour, the one his page called *Ribera*, and the other *Fuentes* his Chamberlaine : and theſe had taken from the Indians ſome skinnes, and ſome mantles, wherewith they were offended, and forſooke their houſes. The Gouernour knew of it, and commanded

them

(marginal notes:)
Saquechuma.

A walled towne.

them to bee apprehended; and condemned to death *Franscisco Osorio*, and the Chamberlaine as principals, and al of them to losse of goods. The Friers and Priests and other principall persons were earnest with him to pardon *Francisco Osorio* his life, & to moderate his sentence, which hee would not grant for any of them. While he was readie to command them to be drawne to the market place to cut off their heads, there came certaine Indians from the Cacique to complaine of them. *Iohn Ortiz*, at the request of *Baltasar de Gallegos* and other persons, changed their words, and told the Gouernour, that the Cacique said, he had notice how his Lordship held those Christians in prison for his sake, and that they were in no sault, neither had they done him any wrong, and that if he would do him any fauour, he should set them free. And he told the Indians; That the Gouernour said, he had them in prison, and that he would punish them in such sort, that they should bee an example to others. Hereupon the Gouerhour commanded the prisoners to be loosed. Assoone as March was come, hee determined to depart from *Chicaça*, and demanded of the Cacique two hundred men for cariages. He sent him answere, that hee would speake with his principall men. Vpon Tuesday the eight of March, the Gouernour went to the towne where he was, to aske him for the men: Hee told him, he would send them the next day. Assoone as the Gouernour was come to *Chicaça*, he told *Luys de Moscoso* the Camp-master, that hee misliked the Indians, and that he should keepe a strong watch that night, which hee remembred but a little. The Indians came at the second watch in foure squadrons, euery one by it selfe, and assoone as they were descried, they sounded

March, 1541.

ded

ded a drum, and gaue the assault with a great cry, and with so great celeritie, that presently they entred with the scoutes, that were somewhat distant from the Campe. And when they were perceiued of them which were in the towne, halfe the houses were on fire, which they had kindled. That night three horsemen chanced to bee skouts, two of them were of base calling, and the worst men in all the Camp, and the other, which was a nephew of the Gouernour, which vntill then was held for a tall man, shewed himselfe there as great a coward, as any of them: for all of them ran away. And the Indians without any resistance came and set the towne on fire; and taried without behind the doores for the Christians, which ran out of the houses, not hauing any leasure to arme themselues; and as they ran hither and thither amazed with the noise, and blinded with the smoke & flame of the fire, they knew not which way they went, neither could they light vpon their weapons, nor saddle their horses, neither saw they the Indians that shot at them. Manie of the horses were burned in the stables, and those which could breake their halters gat loose. The disorder and flight was such, that euery man fled which way he could, without leauing any to resist the Indians. But God, (which chastiseth his according to his pleasure, and in the greatest necessities and dangers sustaineth them with his hand,) so blinded the Indians, that they saw not what they had done, and thought that the horses which ran loose, were men on horsebacke, that gathered themselues together to set vpon them. The Gouernour only rod on horsebacke, and with him a souldier called *Tapia*, and set vpon the Indians, and striking the first he met with his lance, the saddle fell with him,

which

Chicaça set on fire by the Indians.

which with haste was euill girded, and so hee fell from
his horse. And all the people that were on foote were
fled to a wood out of the towne, and there assembled
themselues together. And because it was night, and
that the Indians thought the horses were men on
horsebacke which came to set vpon them, as I said before, they fled; and one onely remained dead, and that
was he whom the Gouernour slew with his lance. The
towne lay all burnt to ashes. There was a woman burned, who, after shee and her husband were both gone
out of their house, went in againe for certaine perles,
which they had forgotten, and when she would haue
come out, the fire was so great at the doore that shee
could not, neither could her husband succour her. O-
ther three Christians came out of their lodgings so
cruelly burned, that one of them died within three
daies, and the other two were carried many daies each
of them vpon a couch betweene staues, which the Indians carried on their shoulders, for otherwise they
could not trauell. There died in this hurliburlie eleuen
Christians, and fiftie horses; and there remained an
hundred hogges, and foure hundred were burned. If
any perchance had saued any clothes from the fire of
Mauilla, here they were burned, and many were clad
in skinnes, for they had no leasure to take their coates.
They endured much cold in this place, and the chiefest remedie were great fires. They spent all night in
turnings without sleepe: for if they warmed one side,
they freesed on the other. Some inuented the wea-
uing of certaine mats of drie iuie, & did weare one beneath, and another aboue: many laughed at this deuice, whom afterward necessitie inforced to doe the
like. The Christians were so spoiled, and in such want

The increase of hogges.

of ſaddles & weapons which were burned, that if the
Indians had come the ſecond night, they had ouercome them with little labour. They remooued thence
to the towne where the Cacique was wont to lie, becauſe it was in a champion countrie. Within eight
daies after, there were many lances and ſaddles made.
There were aſhtrees in thoſe parts, wherof they made
as good lances as in Biſcay.

*The towne
where the Ca-
cique lay.*

Aſhtrees.

Chap. XXI.

*How the Indians ſet againe vpon the Chriſtians, and how
the Gouernour went to* Alimamu, *beyond which
towne in warlike ſort they tarried for him in the
way.*

Pon Wedneſday the 15. of March 1541.
after the Gouernour had lodged 8. daies
in a plaine, halfe a league from the place
which he had wintered in, after he had ſet
vp a forge, and tempered the ſwords which in *Chicaça*
were burned, and made many targets, ſaddles, and lances, on Tueſday night, at the morning watch, many Indians came to aſſault the Campe in three ſquadrons,
euery one by themſelues : Thoſe which watched gaue
the alarme. The Gouernour with great ſpeed ſet his
men in order in other three ſquadrons, and leauing
ſome to defend the Campe, went out to incounter
them. The Indians were ouercome and put to flight.
The ground was champion and fit for ẙ Chriſtians to
take the aduantage of them ; and it was now breake of
day. But there happened a diſorder, whereby there
were not paſt thirtie or fortie Indians ſlaine : and this
it was : that a Frier cried out in the Campe without
any

any iuſt occaſion, To the Campe, To the Campe: Whereupon the Gouernour and all the reſt repaired thither, and the Indians had time to ſaue themſelues. There were ſome taken, by whom the Gouernour informed himſelfe of the Countrie, through which hee was to paſſe. The 25. of Aprill, he departed from *Chicaça*, and lodged at a ſmall towne called *Alimamu.* They had very little Maiz, and they were to paſſe a deſert of ſeuen daies iournie. The next day, the Gouernour ſent three Captaines euerie one his way with horſemen and footemen to ſeeke prouiſion to paſſe the deſert. And *Iohn Dannuſco* the Auditor went with fifteene horſemen, and 40. footemen that way that the Gouernour was to goe, and found a ſtrong fort made, where the Indians ſtaied for him, and many of them walked on the top of it with their weapons, hauing their bodies, thighes and armes okered and died with blacke, white, yellow and red, ſtriped like vnto panes, ſo that they ſhewed as though they went in hoſe and doublets: and ſome of them had plumes, and others had hornes on their heads, and their faces blacke, and their eies done round about with ſtrakes of red, to ſeeme more fierce. Aſſoone as they ſaw that the Chriſtians approched, with a great crie ſounding two drummes with great furie they ſallied foorth to receiue them. *Iohn Dannuſco* and thoſe that were with him, thought good to auoid them, and to acquaint the Gouernour therewith. They retired to a plaine place, a croſſebowſhot from the fort in ſight of it, the footemen, the croſſebowmen, and targetters placed themſelues before the horſemen, that they might not hurt the horſes. The Indians ſallied out by ſeuen and ſeuen, and eight and eight to ſhoote their arrowes, and retired

25. of Aprill.

Alimamu.

Blacke, white, yellow and red colours.

red

red againe: and in sight of the Christians they made a fire, and tooke an Indian, some by the feete, and some by the head, and made as though they went to cast him into the fire, and gaue him first many knocks on the head: signifying, that they meant so to handle the Christians. *Iohn Danusco* sent three horsemen to aduertise the Gouernour hereof. He came presently: for his intent was to driue them from thence, saying, that if he did it not, they would be emboldned to charge him another time, when they might doe him more harme. He made the horsemen to alight, and set his men in foure squadrons: The signe being giuen, they set vp the Indians, which made resistance till the Christians came neere the fort, and assoone as they saw they could not defend theselues, by a place where a brooke passed neere the fort, they ran away, and from the otherside they shot some arrowes: and because at that instant we knew no ford for the horses to passe, they had time enough to get out of our danger. Three Indians were slaine there, and many Christians were hurt, whereof within few daies, there died fifteene by the way. All men thought the Gouernour to bee in fault, because he sent not to see the disposition of the place on the other side of the Riuer, and to know the passage before hee set vpon them. For with the hope they had to saue themselues by flight that way, when they saw none other meanes, they fought til they were broken, and it was an incouragement to defend themselues vntill then, and to offend the Christians without any danger to themselues.

Chap. XXII.
How the Gouernour went from Alimamu *to* Quizquiz, *and from thence to* Rio Grande, *or the great Riuer.*

Hree daies after they had sought some Maiz, whereof they found but little store, in regard of that which was needfull, and that for this cause, as well for their sakes that were wounded, it was needfull for them to rest, as for the great iournie they were to march to come where store of Maiz was: yet the Gouernour was inforced to depart presentlie toward *Quizquiz.* He trauelled seuen daies through a desert ·A desert of of many marishes and thicke woods: but it might all ·seuen daies. be trauelled on horsebacke, except some lakes which they swamme ouer. Hee came to a towne of the Prouince of *Quizquiz* without being descried, and tooke ·A towne of all the people in it before they came out of their hou- ·Quizquiz. ses. The mother of the Cacique was taken there: and he sent vnto him by an Indian, that he should come to see him, and that he would giue him his mother, and al the people which he had taken there. The Cacique sent him answere againe, that his Lordship should loose and send them to him, and that he would come to visit and serue him. The Gouernour, because his people for want of Maiz were somewhat weake and wearie, and the horses also were leane, determined to accomplish his request, to see if hee could haue peace with him, and so commanded to set free his mother and all the rest, and with louing words dismissed them and sent them to him. The next day, when the Gouernour expected the Cacique, there came many In-

N   dians

dians with their bowes and arrowes with a purpose to set vpon the Christians. The Gouernor had commanded all the horsemen to be armed, and on horsebacke, and in a readines. When the Indians saw that they were readie, they staied a crossebow shot from the place where the Gouernour was neere a brooke. And after halfe an houre that they had stood there stil, there came to the Camp sixe principall Indians, and said,

An old prophecie.

they came to see what people they were, and that long agoe, they had been informed by their forefathers,
» That a white people should subdue them: and that
» therefore they would returne to their Cacique, and
» bid him come presently to obey and serue the Gouer-
» nour: and after they had presented him with sixe or seuen skinnes and mantles which they brought, they tooke their leaue of him, and returned with the other, which waited for them by the brookes side. The Cacique neuer came againe nor sent other message. And

Another towne.

because in the towne where the Gouernour lodged, there was small store of Maiz, he remooued to another

Rio Grande, or Rio de Espiritu Santo.

halfe a league from *Rio Grande*, where they found plentie of Maiz: And he went to see the Riuer, and found, that neere vnto it was great store of timber to make barges, and good situation of ground to incampe in. Presently he remooued himselfe thither. They made houses, and pitched their Campe in a plaine field a crossebow shot from the Riuer. And thither was gathered all the Maiz of the townes, which they had latelie passed. They began presently to cut and hew down timber, and to saw plankes for barges. The Indians came presently down the Riuer: they leaped on shore,

Aquixo, a great Lord on

and declared to ẙ Gouernor, That they were subiects of a great Lord, whose name was *Aquixo*, who was

Lord

Lord of many townes, and gouerned many people on the Weſtſide of Rio grande. the other ſide of the Riuer, and came to tell him on his behalſe, that the next day he with al his men would come to ſee, what it would pleaſe him to command him. The next day with ſpeed, the Cacique came with two hundred canoes full of Indians with their bowes and arrowes, painted, and with great plumes of white feathers, and many other colours, with ſhields in their hands, wherewith they defended the rowers on both ſides, and the men of warre ſtood from the head to the ſterne, with their bowes and arrowes in their hands. The canoe wherein the Cacique was, had a tilt ouer the ſterne, and hee ſate vnder the tilt; and ſo were other canoes of the principall Indians. And from vnder the tilt where the chiefe man ſat, hee gouerned and commanded the other people. All ioyned toge-ther, and came within a ſtones caſt of the ſhore. From thence the Cacique ſaid to the Gouernour, which walked along the Riuers ſide with others that waited on him, that he was come thither to viſit, to honour, and to obey him; becauſe he knew he was the greateſt and mightieſt Lord on the earth: therefore he would ſee what he would command him to doe. The Gouer-nour yeelded him thankes, and requeſted him to come on ſhore, that they might the better communicate to-gether. And without any anſwere to that point, hee ſent him three canoes, wherein was great ſtore of fiſh and loaues, made of the ſubſtance of prunes like vnto brickes. After he had receiued al, he thanked him, and prayed him againe to come on ſhore. And becauſe the Caciques purpoſe was, to ſee if with diſſimulation he might doe ſome hurt, when they ſaw that the Go-uernour and his men were in readineſſe, they began to

Two hundred canoes.

Loues made of prunes.

goe

goe from the shore: and with a great crie, the crossebowmen which were ready, shot at them, and slue fiue
or sixe of them. They retired with great order: none
did leaue his oare, though the next to him were slaine;
and shielding themselues, they went farther off. Afterward they came many times and landed: and when
any of vs came toward them, they fled vnto their canoes, which were verie pleasant to behold: for they
were very great and well made, and had their tilts,
plumes, paueses, and flagges, and with the multitude of
people that were in them, they seemed to be a faire armie of gallies. In thirtie daies space, while the Gouernour remained there, they made foure barges: In
three of which hee commanded twelue horsemen to
enter, in each of them foure; in a morning, three houres
before day, men which hee trusted would land in de-
spight of the Indians, and make sure the passage, or die,
and some footemen being crossebowmen went with
them, and rowers to set them on the other side. And
in the other barge he commanded *Iohn de Guzman* to
passe with the footemen, which was made Captaine
in stead of *Francisco Maldonado.* And because the
streame was swift, they went a quarter of a league vp
the Riuer along the bancke, and crossing ouer, fell
downe with the streame, and landed right ouer against
the Camp. Two stones cast before they came to land,
the horsemen went out of the barges on horsebacke to
a sandie plot very hard and cleere ground, where all of
them landed without any resistance. Assoone as those
that passed first, were on land on the other side, the barges returned to the place where the Gouernour was:
and within two houres after Sunne-rising, all the people were ouer. The Riuer was almost halfe a league
　　　　　　　　　　　　　　　　　　　　broad.

Goodly great canoes. *(margin note)*

Foure barges made. *(margin note)*

They passe ouer Rio Grande. The Riuer here almost halfe a league broad. *(margin note)*

broad. If a man stood still on the other side, it could not be discerned, whether he were a man or no. The Riuer was of great depth, and of a strong current: the water was alwaies muddie: there came downe the Riuer continually many trees and timber, which the force of the water and streame brought downe. There was great store of fish in it of sundrie sorts, and the most of it differing from the freshwater fish of *Spaine*, as hereafter shall be shewed.

Chap. XXIII.

How the Gouernour departed from Aquixo *to* Casqui, *and from thence to* Pacaha: *and how this Countrie differeth from that which we had passed.*

Auing passed *Rio grande*, the Gouernour trauelled a league and an halfe, and came to a great towne of *Aquixo*, which was dispeopled before hee came thither. They espied thirtie Indians comming ouer a plaine, which the Cacique sent, to discouer the Christians determination: and assoone as they had sight of them, they tooke themselues to flight. The horsemen pursued them, and slue tenne, and tooke fifteene. And because the towne, whither the Gouernour went, was neere vnto the Riuer, he sent a Captaine, with as many men as he thought sufficient to carrie the barges vp the Riuer. And because in his trauelling by land many times he went farre from the Riuer to compasse the creekes that came from it, the Indians tooke occasion to set vpon them of the barges, and put them in great danger, because that by reason of the great current, they durst not leaue the shore, and from the bancke they shot at

them.

them. Aſſoone as the Gouernour was come to the towne, hee preſently ſent croſſebow men downe the Riuer, which came to reſcue them: and vpon the comming of the barges to the towne, hee commanded them to bee broken, and to ſaue the iron for others, when it ſhould bee needfull. Hee lay there one night, and the day following, hee ſet forward to ſeeke a Prouince, called *Pacaha:* which hee was informed to bee neere vnto *Chiſca,* where the Indians told him there was gold. He paſſed through great townes of *Aquixo,* which were all abandoned for feare of the Chriſtians. Hee vnderſtood by certaine Indians that were taken, that three daies iournie from thence dwelt a great Cacique, whoſe name was *Caſqui.* Hee came to a ſmall Riuer, where a bridge was made, by which they paſſed: that day till Sunſet, they went all in water, which in ſome places came to the waſte, and in ſome to the knees. When they ſaw themſelues on dry land, they were very glad, becauſe they feared they ſhould wander vp and downe as forlorne men al night in the water. At noone they came to the firſt towne of *Caſqui:* they found the Indians careleſſe, becauſe they had no knowledge of them. There were many men and women taken, and ſtore of goods, as mantles and skinnes, as well in the firſt towne, as in another, which ſtood in a field halfe a league from thence in ſight of it, whither the horſemen ran. This Countrie is higher, drier, and more champion, then any part bordering neere the Riuer, that vntill then they had ſeene. There were in the fields many Walnut trees, bearing ſoft ſhelled Walnuts in faſhion like bullets, and in the houſes they found many of them, which the Indians had laid vp in ſtore. The trees differed in nothing elſe from
                    thoſe

A towne.

Pacaha neere vnto Chiſca.
Great townes.

The firſt towne of Caſ-qui.

Another towne.

Walnut trees with ſoft ſhels.

those of *Spaine,* nor from those which we had seene before, but onely that they haue a smaller leafe. There were many Mulberrie trees and Plum trees, which bare red plums like those of *Spaine,* and other gray, somewhat differing, but farre better. And all the trees are all the yeere so fruitfull, as if they were planted in orchards: and the woods were verie thinne. The Gouernour trauelled two daies through the Countrie of *Casqui,* before hee came to the towne where the Cacique was: and the most of the way was alway by champion ground, which was full of great townes, so that from one towne, you might see two or three. He sent an Indian to certifie the Cacique, that hee was comming to the place where hee was, with intent to procure his friendship, and to hold him as his brother. Whereunto he answered, That he should be welcome, and that he would receiue him with speciall good wil, and accomplish all that his Lordship would command him. Hee sent him a present vpon the way; to wit, skinnes, mantles, and fish: And after these complements, the Gouernour found all the townes, as he passed, inhabited with people, which peaceablie attended his comming, and offered him skinnes, mantles, and fish. The Cacique accompanied with many Indians came out of the towne, and staied halfe a league on the way to receiue the Gouernour, and when hee came to him, he spake these words following:

Right high, right mighty, and renowned Lord, your Lordship is most hartilie welcome. Assoone as I had notice of your Lordship, of your power, and your perfections, although you came into my Countrie, killing and taking captiues the inhabitants thereof and my subiects: yet I determined to conforme my will vnto yours, and as your owne to interpret in good part

all

Many Mulberrie trees and plum trees.

Many great townes.

all that your Lordship did : beleeuing, that it was conuenient it should be so for some iust respect, to preuent some future matter reuealed vnto your Lordship, and concealed from me. For well may a mischiefe be permitted to auoid a greater, and that good may come thereof : which I beleeue will so fall out. For it is no reason to presume of so excellent a Prince, that the nobleneße of his heart, and the effect of his will would permit him to suffer any vniust thing. My abilitie is so small to serue you as your Lordship deserueth, that if you respect not mine abundant good will, which humblie offereth all kind of seruice, I deserue but little in your presence. But if it bee reason that this be esteemed, receiue the same, my selfe, my Countrie, and subiects for yours, and dispose of me and them at your pleasure. For if I were Lord of all the world, with the same good will should your Lordship by me be receiued, serued and obeyed.

The Gouernour answered him to the purpose, and satisfied him in few words. Within a while after both of them vsed words of great offers & courtesie the one to the other, and the Cacique requested him to lodge in his houses. The Gouernour, to preserue the peace the better, excused himselfe, saying, that hee would lodge in the fields. And because it was very hot, they camped neere certaine trees a quarter of a league from the towne. The Cacique went to his towne, and came againe with many Indians singing. Assoone as they came to the Gouernour, all of them prostrated themselues vpon the ground. Among these came two Indians that were blind. The Cacique made a speech: to auoid tediousnesse, I will onely tell in few words the substance of the matter. Hee said, that seeing the Gouernour was the sonne of the Sunne, and a great Lord, he besought him to doe him the fauour to giue sight

The chiefe towne of the Cacique of Casqui.

to

to thofe two blind men. The blind men rofe vp prefently, and very earneftly requefted the fame of the
Gouernour. He anfwered, That in the high heauens
was he that had power to giue them health, and whatfoeuer they could aske of him ; whofe feruant he was:
And that this Lord made the heauens and the earth,
and man after his owne likeneffe, and that he fuffered
vpon the croffe to faue mankind, and rofe againe the
third day, and that he died as he was man, and as touching his diuinitie, he was, and is immortall ; and that
he afcended into heauen, where he ftandeth with his
armes open to receiue all fuch as turne vnto him : and
ftraightway he commanded him to make a verie high
croffe of wood, which was fet vp in the higheft place
of the towne ; declaring vnto him, that the Chriftians
worfhipped the fame in refemblance and memorie of
that whereon Chrift fuffered. The Gouernour and
his men kneeled downe before it, and the Indians did
the like. The Gouernour willed him, that from thencefoorth hee fhould worfhip the fame, and fhould aske
whatfoeuer they ftood in need of, of that Lord that he
told him was in heauen. Then he asked him how far
it was from thence to *Pacaha* : He faid, one daies iournie, and that at the end of his Countrie, there was a
lake like a brooke which falleth into *Rio Grande,* and
that hee would fend men before to make a bridge
whereby he might paffe. The fame day that the Gouernour departed thence, he lodged at a towne belonging to *Cafqui* : and the next day hee paffed in fight of
other townes, and came to the lake, which was halfe a
croffebow fhot ouer, of a great depth and current. At
the time of his comming, the Indians had made an

A towne be-
longing to
Cafqui.
Other towns.

O   end

end of the bridge, which was made of timber, laid one tree after another: and on one side it had a course of stakes higher then the bridge, for them that passed to take hold on. The Cacique of *Casqui* came to the Gouernour, and brought his people with him. The Gouernour sent word by an Indian to the Cacique of *Pacaha*, that though hee were enemie to the Cacique of Casqui, and though hee were there, yet he would doe him no disgrace nor hurt, if he would attēd him peaceablie, and embrace his friendship; but rather would intreate him as a brother. The Indian, which the Gouernour sent, came againe, and said, that the Cacique made none account of that which hee told him, but fled with all his men out at the other side of the towne. Presentlie the Gouernour entred, and ran before with the horsemen, that way, by which the Indians fled; and

Another towne.

at another towne distant a quarter of a league from thence, they tooke many Indians: and assoone as the horsemen had taken them, they deliuered them to the Indians of *Casqui*, whom, because they were their enemies, with much circumspection and reioycing, they brought to the towne where the Christians were: and the greatest griefe they had, was this, that they could not get leaue to kill them. There were found in the

Mantles, Deeres skins, Lions skinnes, Beares skins, and Cats skinnes.

towne many mantles, and Deere skinnes, Lions skins, and Beares skinnes, and many Cats skins. Many came so farre poorely apparrelled, and there they clothed themselues: of the mantles, they made them cotes and cassocks, and some made gownes, and lined them with Cats skins; and likewise their cassocks. Of the Deeres skinnes, some made them also ierkins, shirts, hose and shooes: and of the Beare skinnes, they made them ve-

rie

ry good clokes: for no water could pierce them. There were targets of raw oxe hides found there; with which hides they armed their horses. _{Targets of raw oxe hides.}

Chap. XXIIII.

How the Cacique of Pacaha came peaceablie to the Gouernour, and the Cacique of Casqui absented himselfe, and came againe to make his excuse, and how the Gouernour made them both friends.

 Pon Wednesday, the 19. of Iune, the Gouernour entred into *Pacaha* : He lodged in the towne, where the Cacique vsed to reside, which was very great, walled, and _{Pacaha, a very great towne beset with towers.} beset with towers, and many loopeholes were in the towers and wall. And in the towne was great store of old Maiz, and great quantitie of new in the fields. Within a league and halfe a league were great townes all walled. Where the Gouernour was lodged, was _{Great walled townes.} a great lake, that came neere vnto the wall: and it entred into a ditch that went round about the towne, wanting but a little to enuiron it round. From the lake to the great Riuer was made a weare by the which the fish came into it; which the Cacique kept for his recreation and sport: with nets, that were found in the _{Nets found.} towne, they tooke as much as they would: and tooke they neuer so much, there was no want perceiued. There was also great store of fish in many other lakes that were thereabout, but it was soft, and not so good as that which came from the Riuer, and the most of it was different from the freshwater fish of *Spaine*. There _{The diuers sorts of excellen fish in Rio Grande,} was a fish which they called Bagres: the third part of it was head, and it had on both sides the gilles, and

O 2   along

along the sides great pricks like very sharpe aules: those of this kind that were in the lakes were as big as pikes: and in the Riuer, there were some of an hundred, and of an hundred and fiftie pounds weight, and many of them were taken with the hooke. There was another fish like barbilles; and another like breames, headed like a delicate fish, called in *Spaine* besugo, betweene red and gray. This was there of most esteeme. There was another fish called a pele fish: it had a snout of a cubit long, and at the end of the vpper lip it was made like a peele. There was another fish like a Westerne shad: And all of them had scales, except the bagres, and the pele fish. There was another fish, which sometimes the Indians brought vs, of the bignes of an hog, they called it the Pereo fish: it had rowes of teeth beneath and aboue. The Cacique of *Casqui* sent many times great presents of fish, mantles, and skinnes. Hee told the Gouernour, that he would deliuer the Cacique of *Pacaha* into his hands. He went to *Casqui*, and sent many canoes vp the Riuer, and came himselfe by land with many of his people. The Gouernour with 40. horsemen, and 60. footemen tooke him along with him vp the Riuer. And his Indians which were in the canoes, discouered where the Cacique of *Pacaha* was in a little Iland, situated betweene two armes of the Riuer. And fiue Christians entred into a canoe, wherein *Don Antonio Osorio* went before, to see what people the Cacique had with him. There were in the Isle fiue or sixe thousand soules. And assoone as they saw them, supposing that the Indians which were in the other canoes were also Christians, the Cacique, and certaine which were in three canoes, which they had there with the̅, fled in great haste to the other side

Fiue or sixe thousand Indians.

of

of the Riuer: The reſt with great feare and danger, lept into the Riuer, where much people was drowned, eſpecially women, and little children. Preſently the Gouernor which was on land, not knowing what had happened to *Don Antonio,* and thoſe that went with him, commanded ẙ Chriſtians with all ſpeed to enter with the Indians of *Caſqui* in the canoes, which were quickly with *Don Antonio* in the little Iſland, where they tooke many men and women, and much goods. Great ſtore of goods, which the Indians had laid vpon hurdles of canes, and rafts of timber to carrie ouer to the other ſide, draue down the riuer, wherewith the Indians of *Caſqui* filled their canoes: and for feare leſt the Chriſtians would take it from them, the Cacique went home with them downe the Riuer, without taking his leaue of the Gouernour: whereupon the Gouernour was highly offended with him: and preſently returning to *Pacaha,* he ouerran the Countrie of *Caſqui* the ſpace of two leagues, where hee tooke twentie or thirtie of his men. And becauſe his horſes were wearie, and he wanted time that day to goe any farther, hee returned to *Pacaha,* with determination within three or foure daies after to inuade *Caſqui.* And preſently he let looſe one of the Indians of *Pacaha,* and ſent word by him to the Cacique, that if hee would haue his friendſhip, he ſhould repaire vnto him, and that both of them would make warre vpon *Caſqui.* And preſently came many Indians that belonged to *Pacaha,* and brought an Indian, in ſtead of the Cacique, which was diſcouered by the Caciques brother which was taken priſoner. The Gouernour wiſhed the Indians that their Maſter himſelfe ſhould come: for hee knew very well that that was not hee, and told them,

that

that they could doe nothing, which he knew not before they thought it. The next day the Cacique came, accompanied with many Indians, and with a present of much fish, skinnes and mantles. He made a speech that all were glad to heare, and concluded, saying, That though his Lordship, without his giuing occasion of offence had done him hurt in his Countrie, and subiects, yet he would not therefore refuse to bee his, and that he would alwaies be at his commandement. The Gouernour commanded his brother to be loosed, and other principall Indians that were taken prisoners. That day came an Indian from the Cacique of *Casqui*, and said, that his Lord would come the next day to excuse himselfe of the error which he had committed, in going away without licence of the Gouernour. The Gouernour willed the messenger to signifie vnto him, that if he came not in his owne person, he would seeke him himselfe, and giue him such punishment as he deserued. The next day with all speede came the Cacique of *Casqui*, and brought a present to the Gouernour of many mantles, skinnes, and fish, and gaue him a daughter of his, saying, that he greatly desired to match his blood with the blood of so great a Lord as he was, and therefore he brought him his daughter, and desired him to take her to his wife. Hee made a long and discreet oration, giuing him great commendations, and concluded, saying, that hee should pardon his going away without licence, for that Crosses sake, which he had left with him: protesting, that hee went away for shame of that which his men had done without his consent. The Gouernour answered him, that hee had chosen a good patrone; and that if he had not come to excuse himselfe, hee had determined to seeke
him,

him, to burne his townes, to kill him and his people, and to destroy his Countrie. To which he replied, saying:

My Lord, I and mine are yours, and my Countrie like-wise is yours: therefore if you had done so, you should haue destroyed your owne Countrie, and haue killed your owne peo-ple: whatsoeuer shall come vnto me from your hand, I will re-ceiue as from my Lord, aswell punishment as reward: And know you, that the fauour which you did me in leauing me the Crosse, I do acknowledge the same to be a very great one, and greater then I haue euer deserued. For you shall vnderstand, that with great droughts, the fields of Maiz of my Countrie were withered; and assoone as I and my people kneeled before the Crosse, and prayed for raine, presently our necessitie was relieued.

The Gouernour made him, and the Cacique of *Pa-caha* friends; and set them with him at his table to dine with him: and the Caciques fell at variance a-bout the seates, which of them should sit on his right hand. The Gouernour pacified them; telling them, that among the Christians, all was one to sit on the one side, or on the other, willing them so to behaue them-selues, seeing they were with him, that no bodie might heare them, and that euery one should sit in the place that first hee lighted on. From thence he sent thirtie horsemen, and fiftie footemen to the Prouince of *Calu-ça*, to see if from thence hee might trauell to *Chisca*, where the Indians said, there was a worke of gold and copper. They trauelled seuen daies iournie through a desert, and returned verie wearie, eating greene plums and stalkes of Maiz, which they found in a poore towne of sixe or seuen houses. From thence forward toward the North; the Indians said, That the Country

Gold and cop-per in Chisca.

A poore towne.

was.

Great store of
Oxen toward
the North of
Pacaha.
This is like
Quiuera.

was very ill inhabited, becaufe it was very cold: And
that there were fuch ftore of Oxen, that they could
keepe no corne for them: that the Indians liued vpon
their flefh. The Gouernor feeing, that toward that part
the Countrie was fo poore of Maiz, that in it they
could not bee fuftained, demanded of the Indians,
which way it was moft inhabited: and they faid, they
had notice of a great Prouince, and a very plentifull
Countrie, which was called *Quigaute,* and that it was
toward the South.

Chap. XXV.

How the Gouernour departed from Pacaha *to* Quigaute, *and to* Coligoa, *and came to* Cayas.

He Gouernour refted in *Pacaha* fortie daies. In all which time the two
Caciques ferued him with great
ftore of fifh, mantles, and skinnes,
and ftroue who fhould doe him
greateft feruice. At the time of his
departure, the Cacique of *Pacaha*
gaue him two of his fifters, faying, that in figne of loue
that he might remember him, he fhould take them for
his wiues: the ones name was *Macanoche,* and the o-
thers *Mochila:* they were well proportioned, tall of
bodie, and well flefhed. *Macanoche* was of a good
countenance, and in her fhape and phyfiognomie
looked like a Ladie: the other was ftrongly made. The
Cacique of *Cafqui* commanded the bridge to be repaired, and the Gouernour returned through his Countrey, and lodged in the field neere his towne, whither
hee came with great ftore of fifh, and two women,

which

The Caciques
towne.

which hee exchanged with two Christians for two shirts. He gaue vs a guide and men for cariages. The Gouernour lodged at a towne of his, and the next day at another neere a Riuer, whither he caused canoes to be brought for him to passe ouer, and with his leaue returned. The Gouernour tooke his iournie toward *Quigaute.* The fourth day of August, he came to the towne, where the Cacique vsed to keep his residencie: on the way he sent him a present of many mantles and skinnes, and not daring to stay for him in the towne, he absented himselfe. The towne was the greatest that was seene in *Florida.* The Gouernour and his people lodged in the one halfe of it: and within few daies, seeing the Indians became liars, he commanded the other halfe to be burned, because it should not bee a shelter for them, if they came to assault him by night, nor an hindrance to his horsemen for the resisting of them. There came an Indian very well accompanied with many Indians, saying, that hee was the Cacique. He deliuered him ouer to the men of his guard to look vnto him. There went and came many Indians, and brought mantles and skinnes. The counterfeit Cacique, seeing so little opportunitie to execute his euill thought, as hee went one day abroad talking with the Gouernour, he shewed him such a paire of heeles, that there was no Christian that could ouertake him, and he leaped into the Riuer, which was a crossebow shot from the towne: and assoone as hee was on the other side, many Indians that were thereabout making a great crie began to shoote. The Gouernour passed presently ouer to them with horsemen and footemen, but they durst not tarrie for him. Going forward on his way, hee came to a towne where the people were fled,

Marginal notes:
A towne of Casqui.
Another towne.
Quigaute.
The fourth of August.
The greatest towne seene in Florida.
A towne.

P

fled,and a little further to a lake,where the horses could not passe, and on the otherside were many women. The footemen passed, and tooke many of them, and much spoile. The Gouernour came to the Camp: And that night was a spie of the Indians taken by them of the watch. The Gouernour asked him, whether he would bring him where the Cacique was? he said, he would. And he went presently to seeke him with twentie horsemen, and fiftie footemen: and after he had sought him a day, and an halfe, hee found him in a strong wood: And a souldiour not knowing him,gaue him a wound on the head; and he cried out, that he should not kill him,saying,that he was the Cacique: so he was taken, & an hundred and fortie of his men with him. The Gouernour came againe to *Quigaute*, and willed him to cause his men to come to serue the Christians: and staying some daies for their comming,and seeing they came not,he sent two Captaines, euery one his way on both sides of the Riuer with horsemen and footemen. They tooke many men and women. Now seeing the hurt which they sustained for their rebellion, they came to see what the Gouernour would command them, and passed to and fro many times, and brought presents of cloth and fish.

Cloth.

The Cacique and his two wiues were in the lodging of the Gouernour loose, and the halbardiers of his guard did keepe them. The Gouernour asked them which way the Countrie was most inhabited? They said, that toward the South downe the Riuer, were great townes and Caciques,which commanded great

Coligoa neere to certaine mountaines Northweft.

Countries, and much people: And that toward the Northweft, there was a Prouince neere to certaine mountaines, that was called *Coligoa*. The Gouernour

and

and all the rest thought good to goe first to *Coligoa*: saying, that peraduenture the mountains would make some difference of soile, and that beyond them there might be some gold or siluer: As for *Quigaute*, *Casqui*, and *Pacaha*, they were plaine Countries, fat grounds, and full of good medowes on the Riuers, where the Indians sowed large fields of Maiz. From *Tascaluca* to *Rio grande*, or the great Riuer, is about 300. leagues: it is a very low Countrie, and hath many lakes. From *Pacaha* to *Quigaute* may bee an hundred leagues. The Gouernour left the Cacique of *Quigaute* in his owne towne: And an Indian, which was his guide, led him through great woods without any way seuen daies iournie through a desert, where, at euery lodging, they lodged in lakes and pooles in verie shold water: there was such store of fish, that they killed them with cudgils; and the Indians which they carried in chaines, with the mud troubled the waters, and the fish being therewith, as it were, astonied, came to the top of the water, and they tooke as much as they listed. The Indians of *Coligoa* had no knowledge of the Christians, &. when they came so neere the towne, that the Indians saw them, they fled vp a Riuer, which passed neere the towne, and some leaped into it; but the Christians went on both sides of the Riuer, and tooke them. There were many men and women taken, and the Cacique with them. And by his commandement within three daies came many Indians with a present of mantles and Deeres skinnes, and two oxe hides: And they reported, that 5. or 6. leagues from thence toward the North, there were many of these oxen, and that because the Countrie was cold, it was euill inhabited: That the best Countrie

Side notes:
A new way to take fish.
Coligoa.
A Riuer.
Two oxe hides.
Store of oxen toward the North.

which

which they knew; the most plentifull, and most inhabited, was a Prouince called *Cayas*, lying toward the south. From *Quiguate* to *Coligoa* may be 40. leagues.

From Quiguate to Coligoa are 40. leagues.

This towne of *Coligoa* stood at the foote of an hill, on the bank of a meane Riuer, of the bignesse of *Cayas*, the Riuer that passeth by *Estremadura*. It was a fat soile and so plentifull of Maiz, that they cast out the old, to bring in the new. There was also great plentie of French beanes and pompions. The French beanes were greater, and better then those of *Spaine*, and likewise the pompions, and being rosted, they haue almost the taste of chestnuts. The Cacique of *Coligoa* gaue a guide to *Cayas*, and staied behind in his owne towne.

The Prouince of Palisema.

Wee trauelled fiue daies, and came to the Prouince of *Palisema*. The house of the Cacique was found couered with Deeres skinnes of diuers colours and works drawne in them, and with the same in manner of carpets was the ground of the house couered. The Cacique left it so, that the Gouernour might lodge in it, in token that he sought peace and his friendship. But hee durst not tarrie his comming. The Gouernour, seeing he had absented himselfe, sent a Captaine with horsemen and footemen to seeke him: Hee found much people, but by reason of the roughnesse of the Countrie, he tooke none saue a few women and children. The towne was little and scattering, and had very little Maiz. For which cause the Gouernour speedilie departed from thence. Hee came to another towne

Tatalicoya.

called *Tatalicoya*, hee carried with him the Cacique thereof, which guided him to *Cayas*. From *Tatalicoya* are foure daies iournie to *Cayas*. When hee came to

Cayas.

Cayas, and saw the towne scattered; hee thought they had told him a lie, and that it was not the Prouince of

Cayas,

Cayas, becaufe they had informed him that it was well inhabited: He threatned the Cacique, charging him to tell him where hee was: and he and other Indians which were taken neere about that place, affirmed that this was the towne of *Cayas*, and the beft that was in that Countrie, and that though the houfes were diftant the one from the other, yet the ground that was inhabited was great, and that there was great ftore of people, and many fields of Maiz. This towne was called *Tanico*: he pitched his Campe in the beft part of it neere vnto a Riuer. The fame day that the Gouernour came thither, he went a league farther with certaine horfemen, and without finding any people, hee found many skinnes in a pathway, which the Cacique had left there, that they might bee found, in token of peace. For fo is the cuftome in that Countrie.

Tanico.

Chap. XXVI.
How the Gouernour difcouered the Prouince of Tulla, *and what happened vnto him.*

He Gouernor refted a moneth in the Prouince of *Cayas*. In which time the horfes fattened and thriued more, then in other places in a longer time, with the great plentie of Maiz and the leaues thereof, which I thinke was the beft that hath been feene, and they dranke of a lake of very hot water, and fomewhat brackifh, and they dranke fo much, that it fwelled in their bellies when they brought them from the watering. Vntill that time the Chriftians wanted falt, and there they made good ftore, which they carried along with them. The Indians doe carrie it to other places

A lake of hot and fomewhat brackifh waring.
Store of falt made at Cayas.

P 3

" to exchange it for skinnes and mantles. They make it
" along the Riuer, which when it ebbeth, leaueth it vp-
" on the vpper part of the fand. And becaufe they can-
" not make it, without much fand mingled with it, they
" throw it into certaine baskets which they haue for
" that purpofe, broad at the mouth, and narrow at the
" bottom, and fet it in the aire vpon a barre, and throw
" water into it, and fet a fmall veffell vnder it, wherein it
" falleth : Being ftrained and fet to boile vpon the fire,
" when the water is fodden away, the falt remaineth in
" the bottome of the pan. On both fides of the Riuer the
" Countrie was full of fowne fields, and there was ftore
of Maiz. The Indians durft not come ouer where wee
were : & when fome of them fhewed themfelues, the
fouldiers that faw them called vnto them; then the Indians paffed the Riuer, and came with them where the
Gouernor was. He asked thé for the Cacique. They
faid, that he remained quiet, but that he durft not fhew
himfelfe. The Gouernour prefently fent him word,
that he fhould come vnto him, and bring him a guide
and an interpretour for his iournie, if he made account
of his friendfhip : and if he did not fo, he would come
himfelfe to feeke him, and that it would bee the worfe
for him. Hee waited three daies, and feeing he came
not, he went to feeke him, and brought him prifoner
with 150. of his men. He asked him, whether hee had
notice of any great Cacique, & which way the Countrie was beft inhabited. Hee anfwered, that the beft
Countrie thereabout was a Prouince toward the
South, a day and an halfes iournie, which was called
Tulla; and that he could giue him a guide, but no interpretour, becaufe the fpeech of that Countrie was
different from his, and becaufe he and his anceftors
had

had alwaies warres with the Lords of that Prouince, therefore they had no commerce, nor vnderstood one anothers language. Immediatly the Gouernour with certaine horsemen, and 50. footemen, departed toward *Tulla*, to see if the Countrie were such, as hee might passe through it with all his companie : and assoone as he arriued there, and was espied of the Indians, the Countrie gathered together, and assoone as 15. and 20. Indians could assemble themselues, they set vpon the Christians : and seeing that they did handle them shrewdly, and that the horsemen ouertooke them when they fled, they gat vp into the tops of their houses, and sought to defend themselues with their arrowes : and being beaten downe from one, they gat vp vpon another. And while our men pursued some, others set vpon them another way. Thus the skirmish lasted so long, that the horses were tired, and they could not make them runne. The Indians killed there one horse, and some were hurt. There were 15. Indians slaine there, and 40. women and boies were taken prisoners. For whatsoeuer Indian did shoot at them, if they could come by him, they put him to the sword. The Gouernour determined to returne toward *Cayas*, before the Indians had time to gather a head ; and presently that euening, going part of $\tilde{y}$ night to leaue *Tulla*, he lodged by the way, and the next day came to *Cayas* : and within three daies after he departed thēce toward *Tulla* with all his companie : He carried the Cacique along with him, and among all his men, there was not one found that could vnderstand the speech of *Tulla*. He staied three daies by the way, and the day that he came thither, he found the towne abandoned : for the Indians durst not tarrie his comming.

But

Margin notes: Tulla.

The Gouernor commeth againe to Tulla with all his companie.

But assoone as they knew that the Gouernour was in *Tulla*, the first night about ȳ morning watch, they came in two squadrons two seuerall waies, with their bowes and arrowes, and long staues like pikes. Assoone as they were descried, both horse and foot sallied out vpon them, where many of the Indians were slaine: And some Christians and horses were hurt: Some of the Indians were taken prisoners, whereof the Gouernour

Indians haue their right hands and noses cut off.

sent sixe to the Cacique, with their right hands and noses cut off: and sent him word, that if he came not to him to excuse and submit himselfe, that hee would come to seeke him, and that hee would doe the like to him, and as many of his as hee could find, as hee had done to those which hee had sent him: and gaue him three daies respit for to come. And this he gaue them to vnderstand by signes, as well as hee could, for there was no interpretour. At the three daies end, there

Oxe hides.

came an Indian laden with Oxe hides. He came weeping with great sobs, and comming to the Gouernour cast himselfe downe at his feete: He tooke him vp, and he made a speech, but there was none that vnderstood him. The Gouernour by signes commanded him, to returne to the Cacique, and to will him, to send him an interpretor, which could vnderstand the men of *Cayas*. The next day came three Indians laden with oxe

Oxe hides.

hides; and within three daies after came 20. Indians, and among them one that vnderstood them of *Cayas*: Who, after a long oration of excuses of the Cacique, and praises of the Gouernour, concluded with this, that he and the other were come thither on the Caciques behalfe, to see what his Lordship would command him to doe, for he was readie at his commandement. The Gouernour and all his companie were verie

rie glad. For in no wise could they trauell without an interpretour. The Gouernour commanded him to be kept safe, and bad him tell the men that came with him, that they shuld returne to the Cacique, and signi-fie vnto him, that he pardoned him for that which was past, and thanked him much for his presents and inter-pretour, which he had sent him, and that he would bee glad to see him, and that he should come the next day to talke with him. After three daies, the Cacique came, and 80. Indians with him : and himselfe and his men came weeping into the Camp, in token of obedience and repentance for the errour passed, after the manner of that Countrie : He brought a present of many oxe hides : which, because the Countrie was cold, were verie profitable, and serued for couerlets, because they were very soft, and wolled like sheepe. Not farre from thence toward the North were many oxen. The Christians saw them not, nor came into the Countrie where they were, because those parts were euill inha-bited, and had small store of Maiz where they were bred. The Cacique of *Tulla* made an oration to the Gouernour, wherein he excused himselfe, and offered him his Countrie, subiects, and person. Aswell this Cacique as the others, and all those which came to the Gouernour on their behalfe, deliuered their message or speech in so good order, that no oratour could vtter the same more eloquentlie.

The Cacique of Tulla.

Many Oxe hides with wooll on them, as soft as sheepes wooll. Goma-ra Histor. Gene-ner. cap. 215. Many Oxen towa ᵈ the North.

The great elo-quence of the Indians.

Q   CHAP.

Chap. XXVII.

How the Gouernour went from Tulla *to* Autiamque, *where he passed the winter.*

He Gouernour enformed himselfe of all the Countrie round about; and vnderstood, that toward the West was a scattered dwelling, and that toward the Southeast were great townes, especially in a Prouince called *Autiamque*, tenne daies iournie from *Tulla*; which might be about 80. leagues; and that it was a plentifull Countrie of Maiz. And because winter came on, and that they could not trauell two or three moneths in the yeere for cold, waters, and snow: and fearing, that if they should stay so long in the scattered dwelling, they could not be susteined; and also because the Indians said, that neere to *Autiamque* was a great water, and according to their relation, the Gouernour thought it was some arme of the Sea: And because he now desired to send newes of himselfe to *Cuba*, that some supplie of men & horses might be sent vnto him: (for it was aboue three yeeres, since *Donna Isabella*, which was in *Hauana*, or any other person in Christendome had heard of him, and by this time he had lost 250. men, and 150. horses) he determined to winter in *Autiamque*, and the next spring, to goe to the sea cost, and make two brigantines, and send one of them to *Cuba*, and the other to *Nueua Espanna*, that that which went in safetie, might giue newes of him: Hoping with the goods which he had in *Cuba*, to furnish himselfe againe, and to attempt the discouery and conquest toward the West: for he had not yet come where

A winter of two or three moneths.

where *Cabeça de Vaca* had been. Thus hauing sent away the two Caciques of *Cayas* and *Tulla*, he tooke his iournie toward *Autiamque*: Hee traueled fiue daies ouer very rough mountaines, and came to a towne called *Quipana*, where no Indians could be taken for the roughnesse of the Countrie: and the towne being betweene hilles, there was an ambush laid, wherewith they tooke two Indians; which told them, that *Autiamque* was sixe daies iournie from thence, and that there was another Prouince toward the South eight daies iournie off, plentifull of Maiz, and very well peopled, which was called *Guahate*. But because *Autiamque* was neerer, and the most of the Indians agreed of it, the Gouernour made his iournie that way. In three daies he came to a towne called *Anoixi*. He sent a Captaine before with 30. horsemen, and 50. footemen, and tooke the Indians carelesse, hee tooke many men and women prisoners. Within two daies after the Gouernour came to another towne called *Catamaya*, and lodged in the fields of the towne. Two Indians came with a false message from the Cacique to know his determination. Hee bad them tell their Lord, that hee should come and speake with him. The Indians returned and came no more, nor any other message from the Cacique. The next day the Christians went to the towne, which was without people: they tooke as much Maiz as they needed. That day they lodged in a wood, and the next day they came to *Autiamque*. They found much Maiz laid vp in store, and French beanes, and walnuts, and prunes, great store of all sorts. They tooke some Indians which were gathering together the stuffe which their wiues had hidden. This was a champion Countrie, and well inhabited. The

Quipana, fiue daies iournie from Tulla.

Guahate.

Anoixi.

Catamaya.

Autiamque sixe daies iournie from Quipana.

Gouer-

Gouernour lodged in the best part of the towne, and commanded presently to make a sense of timber round about the Campe distant from the houses, that the Indians might not hurt them without by fire. And measuring the ground by pases, hee appointed euery one his part to doe according to the number of Indians which he had : presently the timber was brought by them; and in three daies there was an inclosure made of very hie and thicke posts thrust into the ground, and many railes laid acrosse. Hard by this

A Riuer.

towne passed a Riuer, that came out of the Prouince of *Cayas*; and aboue and beneath it was very well peopled. Thither came Indians on the Caciques behalfe with a present of mantles and skinnes; and an halting Cacique, subiect to the Lord of *Autiamque*, Lord of a

Tietiquaquo.

towne called *Tietiquaquo*, came many times to visit the Gouernour, and to bring him presents of such as hee had. The Cacique of *Autiamque* sent to know of the Gouernour, how long time hee meant to stay in his Countrie? And vnderstanding that he meant to stay aboue three daies, he neuer sent any more Indians, nor any other message, but conspired with the lame Cacique to rebell. Diuers inrodes were made, wherein there were many men and women taken, and the lame Cacique among the rest. The Gouernour respecting the seruices which he had receiued of him, reprehended and admonished him, and set him at libertie, and gaue him two Indians to carrie him in a chaire vpon their shoulders. The Cacique of *Autiamque* desiring to thrust the Gouernour out of his Countrie, set spies ouer him. And an Indian comming one night to the gate of the inclosure, a souldier that watched espied him, and stepping behind the gate, as he came in,

he

he gaue him such a thrust, that he fell downe; and so he carried him to the Gouernour: and as hee asked him wherefore he came, not being able to speake, hee fell downe dead. The night following the Gouernor commanded a souldiour to giue the alarme, and to say that he had seene Indians, to see how ready they would be to answere the alarme. And hee did so sometimes as well there, as in other places, when he thought that his men were carelesse, & reprehended such as were slacke. And as well for this cause, as in regard of doing their dutie, when the alarme was giuen, euery one sought to be the first that should answere. They staied in *Autiamque* three moneths with great plentie of Maiz, French beanes, Walnuts, Prunes, and Conies: which vntill that time they knew not how to catch. And in *Autiamque* the Indians taught them how to take them: which was, with great sprindges, which lifted vp their feete from the ground: And the snare was made with a strong string, whereunto was fastened a knot of a cane, which ran close about the neck of the conie, because they should not gnaw the string. They tooke many in the fields of Maiz, especiallie when it freesed or snowed. The Christians staied there one whole moneth so inclosed with snow, that they went not out of the towne: and when they wanted firewood, the Gouernour with his horsemen going and comming many times to the wood, which was two crossebow shot from the towne, made a pathway, whereby the footemen went for wood. In this meane space, some Indians which went loose, killed many conies with their giues, and with arrowes. These conies were of two sorts, some were like those of *Spaine,* and the other of the same colour and fashion,

Great proui-dence.

Three mo-neths abode in Autiamque.

Frost and snow.

A moneth of snow.

Conies of two sorts.

Q 3   and

and as big as great Hares, longer, and hauing greater loines.

Chap. XXVIII.
How the Gouernour went from Autiamque to Nilco, and from thence to Guacoya.

March 6.
1542.

Pon Monday the sixt of March 1542, the Gouernour departed from *Autiamque* to seeke *Nilco*, which the Indians said was neere the Great riuer, with determination to come to the Sea, and procure some succour of men and horses : for hee had now but three hundred men of warre, and fortie horses, and some of them lame, which did nothing but helpe to make vp the number : and for want of iron they had gone aboue a yeere vnshod : and because they were vsed to it in the plaine countrie, it did them no great harme. *Iohn Ortiz* died in *Autiamque;* which grieued the Gouernor very much : because that without an Interpretour hee feared to enter farre into the land, where he might be lost. From thence forward a youth that was taken in *Cutifachiqui* did serue for Interpretour, which had by that time learned somewhat of the Christians language. The death of *Iohn Ortiz* was so great a mischiefe for the discouering inward, or going out of the land, that to learne of the Indians, that which in foure words hee declared, they needed a whole day with the youth : and most commonly hee vnderstood quite contrarie that which was asked him : whereby it often happened that the way that they went one day, and sometimes two or three daies, they turned backe, and went

astray

The death of Iohn Ortiz, and the great misse of him being their interpretour.

aftray through the wood here and there. The Gouernour fpent ten daies in trauelling from *Autiamque* to a prouince called *Ayays*; and came to a towne that ftood neere the Riuer that paffeth by *Cayas* and *Autiamque*. There hee commanded a barge to be made, wherewith he paffed the Riuer. When he had paffed the Riuer there fell out fuch weather, that foure daies he could not trauell for fnow. Affoone as it gaue ouer fnowing, he went three daies iourney through a Wilderneffe, and a countrie fo low, and fo full of lakes and euill waies, that hee trauelled one time a whole day in water, fometimes knee deepe, fometimes to the ftirrup, and fomtimes they fwamme. He came to a towne called *Tutelpinco*, abandoned, and without Maiz: there paffed by it a lake, that entred into the riuer, which carried a great ftreame and force of water. Fiue Chriftians paffing ouer it in a periagua, which the Gouernour had fent with a Captaine, the periagua ouerfet : fome tooke hold on it, fome on the trees that were in the lake. One *Francis Sebaftian*, an honeft man of *Villa noua de Barca Rota*, was drowned there. The Gouernour went a whole day along the lake feeking paffage, and could finde none, nor any way that did paffe to the other fide. Comming againe at night to the towne hee found two peaceable Indians, which fhewed him the paffage, and which way hee was to goe. There they made of canes and of the timber of houfes thatched with canes, rafts wherewith they paffed the lake. They trauelled three daies, and came to a towne of the territorie of *Nilco*, called *Tianto*. There they tooke thirtie Indians, and among them two principall men of this towne. The Gouernour fent a Captaine with horfemen and footmen before to *Nilco*, becaufe the Indians
might

Margin notes:

Ayays.
A Riuer.

Great fnow about the twentith of March.

Tutelpinco.

A great lake.

Rafts wherewith they paffed the lake.

Tianto.

might haue no time to carrie away the prouision. They passed through three or foure great townes; and in the towne where the Cacique was resident, which was two leagues from the place where the Gouernour remained, they found many Indians with their bowes and arrowes, in manner as though they would haue staied to fight, which did compasse the towne ; and assoone as they saw the Christians come neere them without misdoubting them, they set the Caciques house on fire, and fled ouer a lake that passed neere the towne, through which the horses could not passe. The next day being Wednesday the 29. of March the Gouernour came to *Nilco:* he lodged with all his men in the Caciques towne, which stood in a plaine field, which was inhabited for the space of a quarter of a league : and within a league and halfe a league were other very great townes, wherein was great store of Maiz, of French beanes, of Walnuts, and Prunes. This was the best inhabited countrie, that was seene in *Florida,* and had most store of Maiz, except *Coça,* and *Apalache.* There came to the campe an Indian accompanied with others, and in the Caciques name gaue the Gouernour a mantle of Marterns skinnes, and a cordon of perles. The Gouernour gaue him a few small Margarites, which are certaine beades much esteemed in *Peru,* and other things, wherewith he was very well contented. He promised to returne within two daies, but neuer came againe : but on the contrarie the Indians came by night in canoes, and carried away all the Maiz they could, and made them cabins on the other side of the Riuer in the thickest of the wood, because they might flee if wee should goe to seeke them. The Gouernour, seeing hee came not at the time appointed,

Three or foure great townes.

March 29.

Nilco.

Verie great townes.

The best Countrie of Florida.

Marterns skinnes.
A cordon of perles.

pointed, commanded an ambush to be laid about certaine store-houses neere the lake, whither the Indians came for Maiz: where they tooke two Indians, who told the Gouernour, that hee which came to visit him, was not the Cacique, but was sent by him vnder pretence to spie whether the Christians were carelesse, and whether they determined to settle in that country or to goe forward. Presently the Gouernour sent a Captaine with footmen and horsemen ouer the riuer; and in their passage they were descried of the Indians, and therefore he could take but tenne or twelue men and women, with whom hee returned to the campe. This Riuer which passed by *Nilco*, was that which passed by *Cayas* and *Autiamque*, and fell into *Rio grande*, or the Great Riuer, which passed by *Pachaha* and *Aquixo* neere vnto the prouince of *Guachoya:* and the Lord thereof came vp the Riuer in canoes to make warre with him of *Nilco*. On his behalf there came an Indian to the Gouernour and said vnto him, That he was his seruant, and prayed him so to hold him, and that within two daies hee would come to kisse his Lordships hands: and at the time appointed he came with some of his principal Indians, which accompanied him, and with words of great offers and courtesie hee gaue the Gouernour a present of many Mantles and Deeres skinnes. The Gouernour gaue him some other things in recompense, and honoured him much. Hee asked him what townes there were downe the Riuer? Hee answered that he knew none other but his owne: and on the other side of the Riuer a prouince of a Cacique called *Quigalta*. So hee tooke his leaue of the Gouernour and went to his owne towne. Within few daies the Gouernour determined to goe to *Guachoya*, to

R learne

learne there whether the Sea were neere, or whether there were any habitation neere, where hee might relieue his companie, while the brigantines were making, which he meant to send to the land of the Christians. As he passed the Riuer of *Nilco*, there came in canoes Indians of *Guachoya* vp the streame, and when they saw him, supposing that he came to seeke them to doe them some hurt, they returned downe the Riuer, and informed the Cacique thereof : who with all his people, spoiling the towne of all that they could carrie away, passed that night ouer to the other side of *Rio grande*, or the great Riuer. The Gouernour sent a Captaine with fiftie men in sixe canoes downe the Riuer, and went himselfe by land with the rest : hee came to **Guachoya.** *Guachoya* vpon Sunday the 17. of Aprill : he lodged in the towne of the Cacique, which was inclosed about, and seated a crossebow shot distant from the Riuer. **Foure names** Here the Riuer is called *Tamalliseu*, and in *Nilco Tapatu*, **of Rio grande.** and in *Coça Mico*, and in the port or mouth *Ri*.

Chap. XXIX.
Of the message which the Gouernour sent to Quigalta, *and of the answere which he returned : and of the things which happened in this time.*

S soone as the Gouernour came to *Guachoya*, hee sent *Iohn Danusco* with as many men as could goe in the canoes vp the Riuer. For when they came downe from *Nilco*, they saw on the other side the Riuer new cabins made. *Iohn Danusco* went and brought the canoes loden with Maiz, French beanes, Prunes, and many loaues

loaues made of the substance of prunes. That day came an Indian to the Gouernor from the Cacique of *Guachoya*, and said, that His Lord would come the next day. The next day they saw many canoes come vp the Riuer, and on the other side of the great Riuer, they assembled together in the space of an houre: they consulted whether they should come or not; & at length concluded to come, and crossed the Riuer. In the came the Cacique of *Guachoya*, and brought with him manie Indians with great store of Fish, Dogges, Deeres skinnes, and Mantles: And assoone as they landed, they went to the lodging of the Gouernour, and presented him their gifts, and the Cacique vttered these words:

Mightie and excellent Lord, I beseech your Lordship to pardon mee the errour which I committed in absenting my selfe, and not tarrying in this towne to haue receiued and serued your Lordship; since, to obtaine this opportunitie of time, was, and is as much as a great victorie to me. But I feared that, which I needed not to haue feared, and so did that which was not reason to do: But as haste maketh waste, and I remoued without deliberation; so, as soone as I thought on it, I determined not to follow the opinion of the foolish, which is, to continue in their errour; but to imitate the wise and discreet, in changing my counsell, and so I came to see what your Lordship will command me to doe, that I may serue you in all things that are in my power.

The Gouernour receiued him with much ioy, and gaue him thankes for his present and offer. He asked him, whether hee had any notice of the Sea. Hee answered, no, nor of any townes downe the Riuer on that side; saue that two leagues from thence was one towne of a principall Indian a subiect of his; and on

R 2 the

the other side of the Riuer, three daies iourney from
thence downe the Riuer, was the Prouince of *Quigalta,* which was the greatest Lord that was in that
Countrie. The Gouernour thought that the Cacique
lied vnto him, to rid him out of his owne townes, and
sent *Iohn Danusco* with eight horsemen downe the Riuer, to see what habitation there was, and to informe
himselfe, if there were any notice of the Sea. Hee trauelled eight daies, and at his returne hee said, that in all
that time he was not able to go aboue 14 or 15 leagues,
because of the great creekes that came out of the Riuer, and groues of canes, and thicke woods that were
along the bancks of the Riuer, and that hee had found
no habitation. The Gouernour fell into great dumps
to see how hard it was to get to the Sea: and worse, because his men and horses euery day diminished, being
without succour to sustaine themselues in the country:
The Gouer-
nor falleth sick
of thought. and with that thought he fell sick. But before he tooke
his bed hee sent an Indian to the Cacique of *Quigalta*
to tell him, that hee was the Childe of the Sunne, and
that all the way that hee came all men obeyed and serued him, that he requested him to accept of his friendship, and come vnto him; for he would be very glad to
see him; and in signe of loue and obedience to bring
something with him of that which in his countrie was
most esteemed. The Cacique answered by the same
Indian:

A most wittie
and stout an-
swere of the
Cacique of
Quigalta. *That whereas he said he was the Child of the Sunne, if he
would drie vp the Riuer he would beleeue him : and touching
the rest, that hee was wont to visit none; but rather that all
those of whom he had notice did visit him, serued, obeyed and
paid him tributes willingly or perforce : therefore if hee desired to see him, it were best he should come thither : that if hee
came*

came in peace, he would receiue him with speciall good will; and if in warre, in like manner hee would attend him in the towne where he was, and that for him or any other hee would not shrinke one foote backe.

By that time the Indian returned with this answere, the Gouernour had betaken himselfe to bed, being euill handled with feuers, and was much aggrieued, that he was not in case to passe presently the Riuer and to seeke him, to see if he could abate that pride of his, considering the Riuer went now very strongly in those parts; for it was neere halfe a league broad, and 16. fathomes deep, and very furious, and ranne with a great current; and on both sides there were many Indians, and his power was not now so great, but that hee had need to helpe himselfe rather by slights then by force. The Indians of *Guachoya* came euery day with fish in such numbers, that the towne was full of them. The Cacique said, that on a certaine night hee of *Quigalta* would come to giue battell to the Gouernour. Which the Gouernour imagined that he had deuised, to driue him out of his countrey, and commanded him to bee put in hold: and that night and all the rest, there was good watch kept. Hee asked him wherefore *Quigalta* came not? He said that hee came, but that he saw him prepared, and therfore durst not giue the attempt: and hee was earnest with him to send his Captaines ouer the Riuer, and that he would aide him with many men to set vpon *Quigalta*. The Gouernour told him that assoone as he was recouered, himselfe would seeke him out. And seeing how many Indians came daily to the towne, and what store of people was in that countrie, fearing they should al conspire together and plot some treason against him; and because the towne had some

open gaps which were not made an end of inclosing,
besides the gates which they went in and out by : because the Indians should not thinke he feared them,
he let them all alone vnrepaired; and commanded the
horsemen to be appointed to them, and to the gates :
and all night the horsemen went the round; and two
and two of euery squadron rode about, and visited the
skouts that were without the towne in their standings
by the passages, and the crossebowmen that kept the
canoes in the Riuer. And because the Indians should
stand in feare of them, hee determined to send a Captaine to *Nilco*, for those of *Guachoya* had told him that
it was inhabited; that by vsing them cruelly, neither
the one nor the other should presume to assaile him;
and hee sent *Nunnez de Touar* with fifteene horsemen,
and *Iohn de Guzman* Captaine of the footmen with his
companie in canoes vp the Riuer. The Cacique of
Guachoya sent for many canoes and many warlike Indians to goe with the Christians : and the Captaine of
the Christians, called *Nunnez de Touar*, went by land
with his horsemen, and two leagues before he came to
Nilco hee staied for *Iohn de Guzman*, and in that place
they passed the Riuer by night : the horsemen came
first, and in the morning by breake of day in sight of
the towne they lighted vpon a spie; which assoone as
he perceiued the Christians, crying out amaine fled to
the towne to giue warning. *Nunnez de Touar* and his
companie made such speed, that before the Indians of
the towne could fully come out, they were vpon them :
it was champion ground that was inhabited, which
was about a quarter of a league. There were about fiue

Fiue or sixe
thousand peo-
ple in Nilco.

or sixe thousand people in the towne : and, as many
people came out of the houses, & fled from one house
to

to another, and many Indians came flocking together from all parts, there was neuer a horseman that was not alone among many. The Captaine had commanded that they should not spare the life of any male. Their disorder was so great, that there was no Indian that shot an arrow at any Christian. The shreekes of women and children were so great, that they made the eares deafe of those that followed them. There were slaine an hundred Indians, little more or lesse: and many were wounded with great wounds, whom they suffered to escape to strike a terror in the rest that were not there. There were some so cruell and butcherlike, that they killed old and young, and all that they met, though they made no resistance: and those which presumed of themselues for their valour, and were taken for such, brake through the Indians, bearing downe many with their stirrops and brests of their horses; and some they wounded with their lances, and so let them goe: and when they saw any youth or woman they tooke them, and deliuered them to the footmen. These mens sinnes by Gods permission lighted on their own " heads: who, because they would seeme valiant, became " cruell; shewing themselues extreme cowards in the " sight of all men, when as most neede of valour was re-" quired, and * afterward they came to a shameful death. *Chap. 37. Of the Indians of *Nilco* were taken prisoners, fourescore women and children, and much spoile. The Indians of *Guachoya* kept back before they came at the towne, and staied without, beholding the successe of the Christians with the men of *Nilco*. And when they saw them put to flight, and the horsemen busie in killing of them, they hastened to the houses to rob, and filled their canoes with the spoile of the goods; and returned

turned to *Guachoya* before the Christians; and won-
dring much at the sharpe dealing which they had
seene them vse toward the Indians of *Nilco*, they told
their Cacique all that had passed with great astonish-
ment.

CHAP. XXX.

Of the death of the Adelantado Fernando de Soto :
And how Luys Moscoso de Aluarado *was elected
Gouernour in his stead.*

HE Gouernour felt in himselfe that
the houre approched, wherein hee
was to leaue this present life, and
called for the Kings officers, Captaines and principall persons, to
whom he made a speech, saying :
*That now he was to goe to giue an account before the pre-
sence of God of all his life past : and since it pleased him to take
him in such a time, and that the time was come that he knew
his death, that he his most vnworthie seruant did yeeld him
many thankes therefore; and desired all that were present
and absent (whom he confessed himselfe to be much beholding
vnto for their singular vertues, loue and loyaltie, which himselfe had well tried in the trauels, which they had suffered,
which alwaies in his mind he did hope to satisfie and reward,
when it should please God to giue him rest, with more prosperitie of his estate,) that they would pray to God for him, that
for his mercie he would forgiue him his sinnes, and receiue his
soule into eternall glorie : and that they would quit and free
him of the charge which hee had ouer them, and ought vnto
them all, and that they would pardon him for some wrongs
which they might haue receiued of him : And to avoid some
diuision,*

diuision, which vpon his death might fall out vpon the choice of his successour, he requested them to elect a principall person, and able to gouerne, of whom all should like well; and when he was elected, they should sweare before him to obey him: and that he would thanke them very much in so doing; because the griefe that he had, would somewhat be asswaged, and the paine that he felt, because he left them in so great confusion, to wit, in leauing them in a strange Countrie, where they knew not where they were.

Baltasar de Gallegos answered in the name of all the rest: And first of all comforting him, he set before his eies how short the life of this world was, and with how many troubles and miseries it is accompanied, and how God shewed him a singular fauor which soonest left it: telling him many other things fit for such a time. And for the last point, that since it pleased God to take him to himselfe, although his death did iustly grieue them much, yet as wel he, as al the rest, ought of necessitie to conforme themselues to the will of God. And touching the Gouernour which he commanded they should elect, he besought him, that it would please his Lordship to name him which he thought fit, and him they would obey. And presently he named *Luys de Moscoso de Aluarado* his Captaine generall. And presently he was sworne by all that were present and elected for Gouernour. The next day, being the 21. of May, 1542. departed out of this life, the valorous, virtuous, and valiant Captaine, *Don Fernando de Soto*, Gouernour of *Cuba*, and Adelantado of *Florida*: whom fortune aduanced, as it vseth to doe others, that hee might haue the higher fal. He departed in such a place, and at such a time, as in his sicknesse he had but little comfort: and the danger wherein all his people were

The death of Don Ferdinando de Soto the 21. of May, 1542 at Guacoya.

S   of

of perishing in that Countrie, which appeared before their eies, was cause sufficient, why euery one of them had need of comfort, and why they did not visit nor accompanie him as they ought to haue done. *Luys de Moscoso* determined to conceale his death from the Indians, because *Ferdinando de Soto* had made them beleeue, That the Christians were immortall; and also because they tooke him to be hardie, wise, and valiant: and if they should know that he was dead, they would bee bold to set vpon the Christians, though they liued peaceablie by them. In regard of their disposition, and because they were nothing constant, and beleeued all that was tolde them, the Adelantado made them beleeue, that he knew some things that passed in secret among themselues, without their knowledge, how, or in what manner he came by them: and that the figure which appeared in a glasse, which he shewed them, did tell him whatsoeuer they practised and went about: and therefore neither in word nor deed durst they attempt any thing that might bee preiudiciall vnto him.

Assoone as he was dead, *Luis de Moscoso* commanded to put him secretly in an house, where hee remained three daies: and remoouing him from thence, commanded him to bee buried in the night at one of the gates of the towne within the wall. And as the Indians had seene him sick, and missed him, so did they suspect what might bee. And passing by the place where hee was buried, seeing the earth mooued, they looked and spake one to another. *Luys de Moscoso* vnderstanding of it, commanded him to be taken vp by night, and to cast a great deale of sand into the mantles, wherein he was winded vp, wherein hee was carried in a canoe,

and

A wittie stratagem.

and throwne into the middeſt of the Riuer. The Cacique of *Guachoya* inquired for him, demanding what was become of his brother and Lord, the Gouernour: *Luys de Moſcoſo* told him, that hee was gon to heauen, as many other times hee did: and becauſe hee was to ſtay there certaine daies, hee had left him in his place. The Cacique thought with himſelfe that he was dead; and commanded two young and well proportioned Indians to be brought thither; and ſaid, that ỹ vſe of that Countrie was, when any Lord died, to kill Indians to wait vpon him, and ſerue him by the way: and for that purpoſe by his commandement were thoſe come thither: and prayed *Luys de Moſcoſo* to command them to be beheaded, that they might attend and ſerue his Lord and brother. *Luys de Moſcoſo* told him, that the Gouernour was not dead, but gone to heauen, and that of his owne Chriſtian ſouldiers, he had taken ſuch as he needed to ſerue him, & praied him to command thoſe Indians to be looſed, and not to vſe any ſuch bad cuſtome from thencefoorth: ſtraightway hee commanded them to be looſed, and to get them home to their houſes. And one of them would not goe; ſaying, that hee would not ſerue him, that without deſert had iudged him to death, but that hee would ſerue him as long as hee liued, which had ſaued his life.

This is alſo the cuſtome of the old Tartars.

Luys de Moſcoſo cauſed all the goods of the Gouernor to be ſold at an outcrie: to wit, two men ſlaues, & two women ſlaues, and three horſes, and 700 hogges. For euery ſlaue or horſe, they gaue two or three thouſand ducats: which were to be paied at the firſt melting of gold or ſiluer, or at the diuiſion of their portion of inheritance. And they entred into bonds, though in the

Seuen hundred hogges.

Countrie

Countrie there was not wherewith, to pay it within a yeere after, and put in sureties for the same. Such as in *Spaine* had no goods to bind, gaue two hundred ducats for an hog, giuing assurance after the same maner. Those which had any goods in *Spaine*, bought with more feare, and bought the lesse. From that time forward, most of the companie had swine, and brought them vp, and fed vpon them; and obserued Fridaies and Saturdaies, and the euenings of feasts, which before they did not. For sometimes in two or three moneths they did eate no flesh, and whensoeuer they could come by it, they did eate it.

Chap. XXXI.

How the Gouernour Luys de Moscoso *departed from* Guachoya, *and went to* Chaguate; *and from thence to* Aguacay.

Ome were glad of the death of *Don Ferdinando de Soto,* holding for certaine, that *Luys de Moscoso* (which was giuen to his ease) would rather desire to be among the Christians at rest, then to continue the labours of the warre in subduing and discouering of Countries; whereof they were alreadie wearie, seeing the small profit that insued thereof. The Gouernour commanded the Captaines and principall persons to meet to consult and determine what they should doe. And being informed what peopled habitation was round about, he vnderstood that to the West, the Countrie was most inhabited, and that downe the Riuer beyond *Quigalta* was vninhabited, and had little store of food.

He

He defired them all, that euerie one would giue his o-
pinion in writing, & fet his hand to it: that they might
refolue by generall confent, whether they fhould goe
downe the Riuer, or enter into the maine land. All
were of opinion, that it was beft to go by land toward Their general
the Weft, becaufe *Nueua Efpanna* was that way; hol- refolution to
ding the voyage by fea more dangerous, and of grea- trauell by
ter hazard, becaufe they could make no fhip of any land Weft-
ftrength to abide a ftorme, neither had they Mafter, nor ward.
Pilot, Compaffe, nor Chart, neither knew they how
farre the fea was off, nor had any notice of it; nor whether the Riuer did make any great turning into the
land, or had any great fall from the rocks, where all of
them might be caft away. And fome which had feene
the fea-chart, did find, that from the place where they
were by the fea coaft to *Noua Efpanna*, might bee 400.
leagues, little more or leffe; and faid, that though they
went fomewhat about by land in feeking a peopled
Countrie, if fome great wildetneffe which they could
not paffe did not hinder thê, by fpending that fommer
in trauell, finding prouifion to paffe the winter in fome
peopled Countrie, that the next fommer after they
might come to fome Chriftian land, and that it might
fortune in their trauel by land to find fome rich Countrie, where they might doe themfelues good. The
Gouernour, although he defired to get out of *Florida*
in fhorter time, feeing the inconueniences they laid
before him, in trauelling by fea, determined to follow
that which feemed good to them all. On Monday the The fifth of
fifth of Iune, he departed from *Guachoya*. The Caci- Iune.
que gaue him a guide to *Chaguate*, and ftaied at home Catalte.
in his owne towne. They paffed through a Prouince
called *Catalte*: and hauing paffed a wilderneffe of fixe
S 3   daies

daies iournie, the twentieth day of ẏ moneth he came to *Chaguate.* The Cacique of this Prouince had visited the Gouernour *Don Ferdinando de Soto* at *Autiamque,* whither he brought him presents of skinnes, and mantles and salt. And a day before *Luys de Moscoso* came to his towne, we lost a Christian that was sicke; which hee suspected that the Indians had slaine. Hee sent the Cacique word, that he should command his people to seeke him vp, and send him vnto him, and that he would hold him, as he did, for his friend: and if he did not, that neither he, nor his, should escape his hands, and that hee would set his Countrie on fire. Presently the Cacique came vnto him, and brought a great present of mantles and skinnes, and the Christian that was lost, and made this speech following:

Right excellent Lord, I would not deserue that conceit which you had of me, for all the treasure of the world. What inforced me to goe to visit and serue the excellent Lord Gouernour you father in Autiamque, *which you should haue remembred, where I offered my selfe with all loyaltie, faith and loue, during my life to serue and obey him? What then could be the cause, I hauing receiued fauours of him, and neither you nor he hauing done me any wrong, that should mooue me to doe the thing, which I ought not? Beleeue this of mee, that neither wrong, nor any worldly interest, was able to make me to haue done it, nor shall be able to blind me. But as in this life it is a naturall course, that after one pleasure, many sorrowes doe follow: so by your indignation, fortune would moderate the ioy, which my heart conceiueth with your presence; and that I should erre, where I thought surest to haue hit the marke; in harboring this Christian which was lost, and vsing him in such manner, as he may tell himselfe, thinking that herein I did you seruice, with purpose to deliuer him*

vnto

vnto you in Chaguate, *and to serue you to the vttermost of my power. If I deserue punishment for this, I will receiue it at your hands, as from my Lord, as if it were a fauour. For the loue which I did beare to the excellent Gouernour, and which I beare to you hath no limit. And like as you giue me chastisement, so will you also shew me fauour. And that which now I craue of you is this, to declare your will vnto me, and those things, wherein I may bee able to doe you the most and best seruice.*

The Gouernour answered him, that because he did not find him in that towne, hee was incensed against him, thinking he had absented himselfe, as others had done: But seeing he now knew his loyaltie and loue, he would alwaies hold him as a brother, and fauour him in all his affaires. The Cacique went with him to the towne where he resided, which was a daies iournie from thence. They passed through a smal town, where there was a lake, where the Indians made salt: and the Christians made some one day while they rested there, of a brackish water, which sprang neere the towne in ponds like fountaines. The Gouernour staied in *Chaguate* sixe daies. There he was informed of the habitation that was toward the West. They told him, that three daies iournie from thence was a Prouince called *Aguacay.* The day that he departed from *Chaguate,* a Christian, called *Francisco de Guzman,* the base sonne of a Gentleman of *Siuill,* staied behind, and went to the Indians, with an Indian woman which he kept as his concubine, for feare he should be punished for gaming debts, that he did owe. The Gouernor had trauelled two daies before he missed him; hee sent the Cacique word to seeke him vp, and to send him to *Aguacay,* whither he trauelled: which hee did not performe.

(margin: A smal towne.)

(margin: Salt made of salt springs of water.)

forme. From the Cacique of *Aguacay,* before they came into the Countrie, there met him on the way 15. Indians with a present of skinnes, fish and rosted venison. The Gouernour came to his towne on Wednesday, the fourth of Iulie. He found the towne without people, and lodged in it: he staied there about a day; during which, he made some roades, and tooke many men and women. There they had knowledge of *the South Sea.* Here there was great store of salt made of sand, which they gather in a vaine of ground like peeble stones. And it was made as they make salt in *Cayas.*

Aguacay.

Knowledge of the South Sea.

Store of Salt made.

Chap. XXXII.
How the Gouernour went from Aguacay to Naguatex, and what happened vnto him.

A smal towne.

THe same day that the Gouernour departed from *Aguacay* he lodged in a small towne subiect to the Lord of that prouince. The Campe pitched hard by a lake of salt water; and that euening they made some salt there. The day following hee lodged betweene two mountaines in a thinne groue of wood. The next day hee came to a small towne called *Pato.* The fourth day after his departure from *Aguacay* he came to the first habitation of a prouince called *Amaye.* There an Indian was taken, which said that from thence to *Naguatex* was a day and a halfes iourney; which they trauelled, finding all the way inhabited places. Hauing passed the peopled countrie of *Amaye,* on Saturday the 20. of Iulie they pitched their Campe at noone betweene *A-*

Salt made here.
Pato.

Amaye.

Iulie 20.

maye

maye and *Naguatex* along the corner of a groue of very faire trees. In the same place certaine Indians were discouered, which came to view them. The horsemen went out to them, and killed six, and tooke two; whom the Gouernour asked, wherefore they came? They said, to know what people hee had, and what order they kept; and that the Cacique of *Naguatex* their Lord had sent them, and that he, with other Caciques which came to aide him, determined that day to bid him battell. While they were occupied in these questions and answeres, there came many Indians by two waies in two squadrons: and when they saw they were descried, giuing a great crie they assaulted the Christians each squadron by it selfe: but seeing what resistance the Christians made them, they turned their backes and betooke themselues to flight, in which many of them lost their liues; and most of the horsemen following them in chase, carelesse of the Camp, other two squadrons of Indians, which lay in ambush, set vpon the Christians that were in the Campe, which also they resisted, who also had their reward as the first. After the flight of the Indians, and that the Christians were retired, they heard a great noise a crossebow shot from the place where they were. The Gouernour sent twelue horsemen to see what it was. They found sixe Christians, foure footmen and two horsemen, among many Indians; the horsemen defending the footmen with great labour. These being of them that chased the first two squadrons, had lost themselues, and comming to recouer the Campe fell among those with whom they were fighting: and so they, and those that came to succour thē, slew many of the Indians, and brought one aliue to the Campe: whom the Gouernour examined,

T   mined,

mined, who they were that came to bid him battell. He told him, that they were the Cacique of *Naguatex*, and of *Amaye*, and another of a prouince called *Haca-* **Hacanac.** *nac*, a Lord of great countries and many subiects; and that the Cacique of *Naguatex* came for Captaine and chiefest of them all. The Gouernour commanded his right arme and nose to be cut off, and sent him to the Cacique of *Naguatex*, charging him to tell him, that the next day hee would bee in his countrey to destroy him; and if hee would withstand his entrance, hee should stay for him. That night he lodged there; and **Naguatex.** the next day hee came to the habitation of *Naguatex*, which was very scattering: he inquired where the Ca-ciques chiefe towne was? They told him that it was **A Riuer.** on the other side of a Riuer, that passed thereby: hee trauelled thitherward, and came vnto it: and on the other side hee saw many Indians, that taried for him, making shew as though they would defend the pas-sage. And because hee knew not whether it could bee waded, nor where the passage was; and that some Christians and horses were hurt; that they might haue time to recouer, he determined to rest certaine daies in the towne where he was. So hee pitched his campe a quarter of a league from the Riuer, because the wea-ther was very hot, neere vnto the towne, in a thinne groue of very faire and hie trees neere a brookes side: and in that place were certaine Indians taken; whom hee examined, whether the Riuer were wadeable or no? They said, yea, at some times, and in some places. **August.** Within ten daies after he sent two Captaines with fif-teene horsemen a peece vpward and downe the Ri-uer with Indians to shew them where they should goe ouer, to see what habitation was on the other side:

And

And the Indians withstood them both, defending the passage of the Riuer as farre as they were able, but they passed in despite of them: and on the other side of the Riuer they saw great habitation, and great store of victuals; and with these newes returned to the Camp.

They passe the Riuer.

Chap. XXXIII.

How the Cacique of Naguatex *came to visite the Gouernour: and how the Gouernour departed from* Naguatex *and came to* Nondacao.

He Gouernour sent an Indian from *Naguatex* where hee lay, to command the Cacique to come to serue and obey him, and that hee would forgiue him all that was past; and if he came not, that he would seeke him, and giue him such punishment as he had deserued for that which he had done against him. Within two daies the Indian returned, & said that the Cacique would come the next day: which, the same day when he came, sent many Indians before him, among whom there were some principall men: hee sent them to see what countenance they found in the Gouernour, to resolue with himselfe whether hee should goe or not. The Indians let him vnderstand, that he was comming, and went away presently: and the Cacique came within two houres accompanied with many of his men: they came all in a ranke one before another on both sides, leauing a lane in the middest where hee came. They came where the Gouernour was, all of them weeping after the manner of *Tulla*, which was not farre from thence toward the East. The Cacique made his due obedience, and this speech following:

Tulla not far from Naguatex, Eastward.

T 2   *Right*

Right high and mightie Lord, whom all the world ought to serue and obey, I was bold to appeare before your Lordship, hauing committed so heinous and abominable an act, as only for me to haue imagined, deserued to be punished; trusting in your greatnes, that although I deserue to obtaine no pardon, yet for your owne sake only you will vse clemencie toward me, considering how small I am in comparison of your Lordship; and not to think vpon my weaknesses, which, to my griefe and for my greater good, I haue knowne. And I beleeue that you and yours are immortall; and that your Lordship is Lord of the land of nature, seeing that you subdue all things, and they obey you, euen the very hearts of men. For when I beheld the slaughter and destruction of my men in the battell, which, through mine ignorāce, and the counsell of a brother of mine, which died in the same, I gaue your Lordship, presently I repented me in my heart of the error, which I had committed; and desired to serue and obey you: and to this end I come, that your Lordship may chastise and command mee as your owne.

The Gouernour answered him, that he forgaue him all which was past, that from thenceforth hee should do his dutie, & that he would hold him for his friend, and that he would fauour him in all things. Within foure daies hee departed thence, and comming to the Riuer he could not passe, because it was growne very bigge; which seemed to him a thing of admiration, being at that time that it was, and since it had not rained a moneth before. The Indians said, that it increased many times after that manner without raining in all the countrie. It was supposed, that it might bee the tide that came into it. It was learned that the flood came alway from aboue, and that the Indians of all that countrie had no knowledge of the Sea. The Go-uernour

The Riuer growne vnpassable in August, at Naguatex.

Coniectures of a Sea to the Northward.

uernour returned vnto the place where he had lodged
before : and vnderstanding within eight daies after
that the Riuer was passeable, he departed. He passed o-
uer and found the towne without people : he lodged A towne.
in the field, and sent the Cacique word to come vnto
him, and to bring him a guide to goe forward. And
some daies being past, seeing the Cacique came not,
nor sent any bodie, hee sent two Captaines sundrie
waies to burne the townes, and to take such Indians as Townes bur-
they could finde : They burnt great store of victuals, ned.
and took many Indians. The Cacique seeing the hurt
that he receiued in his countrie, sent sixe principall Indians with three men for guides, which knew the language of the countrie, through which the Gouernour
was to passe. Hee departed presently from *Naguatex*,
and within three daies iourney came to a towne of
foure or fiue houses, which belonged to the Cacique
of that prouince, which is called *Nissoone* : it was euill Nissoone.
inhabited and had little Maiz. Two daies iourney forward the guides which guided the Gouernour, if they
were to goe Westward, guided him to the East ; and
sometimes went vp and downe through very great
woods out of the way. The Gouernour commanded
them to bee hanged vpon a tree : and a woman that
they tooke in *Nissoone* guided him, and went backe
againe to seeke the way. In two daies he came to another miserable towne, called *Lacane* : an Indian was ta- Lacane.
ken in that place, that said, that the countrie of *Nonda-* Nondacao.
cao was a countrie of great habitation, and the houses
scattering the one from the other, as they vse to bee in
mountains, and had great store of Maiz. The Cacique
came with his men weeping, like them of *Naguatex* :
for this is their vse in token of obedience : hee made

him

him a present of much fish, and offered to doe what he would command him. Hee tooke his leaue, and gaue him a guide to the prouince of *Soacatino.*

Chap. XXXIIII.

How the Gouernour went from Nondacao *to* Soacatino *and* Guasco, *and passed through a desert, from whence, for want of a guide, and an interpretour, he returned to* Nilco.

He Gouernour departed from *Nondacao* toward *Soacatino,* and in fiue daies iournie came to a Prouince called *Aays.* The Indians which inhabited it, had no notice of the Christians: but assoone as they saw that they entred into their country, they assembled themselues : and as they came together 50. or 100. they came foorth to fight: while some fought, others came and charged our men another way, and while they followed some, others followed them. The fight lasted the greatest part of the day, till they came to their towne. Some horses and men were wounded, but not to any hurt of their trauelling : for there was no wound that was dangerous. There was a great spoile made of the Indians. That day that the Gouernour departed from thence, the Indian that guided him said, that in *Nondacao* he had heard say, that the Indians of *Soacatino* had seene other Christians, whereof they all were very glad : thinking it might be true, and that they might haue entred into those parts by *Nueua Espanna;* and that if it were so, it was in their owne hand to goe out of *Florida,* if they found nothing

Aays.

A towne.

thing of profit : for they feared they should lose themselues in some wildernes. This Indian led him two
daies out of the way. The Gouernour commanded to
torture him. He said, that the Cacique of *Nondacao,* his
Lord, had commanded him to guide them so, because
they were his enemies, and that hee was to doe as his
Lord commanded him. The Gouernour commanded
him to be cast to the dogs : and another guided him
to *Soacatino,* whither hee came the day following. It Soacatino.
was a verie poore Countrie : there was great want of
Maiz in that place. Hee asked the Indians, whether
they knew of any other Christians. They said, that a
little from thence toward the South they heard they
were. He trauelled 20. daies through a Countrie euill 20. daies tra-
inhabited, where they suffered great scarcitie and trou- uell toward
ble. For that little Maiz which the Indians had, they the South.
had hidden and buried in the woods, where the Christians, after they were well wearied with their trauell,
at the end of their iournie went to seeke by digging
what they should eat. At last, comming to a Prouince
that was called *Guasco,* they found Maiz, wherewith Guasco : here
they loaded their horses, and the Indians that they they found
had. From thence they went to another towne called stones, and
Naquiscoça. The Indians said, they had no notice of mantles of
any other Christians. The Gouernour commanded Chap. 35.
to torment them. They said, that they came first to a- Naquiscoça.
nother Lordship, which was called *Naçacahoz,* and Naçacahoz.
from thence returned again to the West, from whence
they came. The Gouernour came in two daies to *Na-*
çacahoz : Some women were taken there : among
whom there was one, which said, that she had seene
Christians, and had been taken by them, and had run
away. The Gouernour sent a Captaine with 15. horsemen

men to the place where the woman said she had seene them, to see if there were any signe of horses, or any token of their being there. After they had gone three or foure leagues, the woman that guided them said, that all that she had told them was vntrue. And so they held all the rest that the Indians had said, of seeing Christians in the land of *Florida*. And, because the Countrie that way was poore of Maiz, and toward the West, there was no notice of any habitation, they returned to *Guasco*. The Indians told them there, that 10. daies iournie from thence toward the West, was a Riuer called *Daycao*; whither they went sometimes a hunting and killing of Deere: and that they had seene people on the other side, but knew not what habitation was there. There the Christians tooke such Maiz as they found and could carrie, and, going 10. daies iournie through a wildernesse, they came to the Riuer which the Indians had told them of. Ten horsemen, which the Gouernour had sent before, passed ouer the same, and went in a way that led to the Riuer, and lighted vpon a companie of Indians that dwelt in verie little cabins: who, assoone as they saw them, tooke themselues to flight, leauing that which they had; all which was nothing but miserie and pouertie. The Countrie was so poore, that among them all there was not found halfe a peck of Maiz. The horsemen tooke two Indians, and returned with them to the Riuer, where the Gouernour staied for them. He sought to learne of them what habitation was toward the West. There was none in the Camp that could vnderstand their language. The Gouernour assembled the Captaines and principall persons, to determine with their aduice what they should doe. And the most

part

They returned to Guasco.

The Riuer of Daycao: which seemeth to be Rio del oro.

part said, that they thought it best to returne backe to *Rio grande*, or the Great Riuer of *Guachoya*; because that in *Nilco* and thereabout was store of Maiz: saying, that they would make pinaces that winter, and the next sommer passe down the Riuer to the seaward in them, and comming to the Sea they would goe along the coast to *Nueua Espanna.* For though it seemed a doubt-full thing and difficult, by that which they had already alleaged, yet it was the last remedie they had. For by land they could not goe for want of an Interpretour. And they held, that the countrie beyond the Riuer of *Daycao*, where they were, was that which *Cabeça de Va-ca* mentioned in his relation that he passed *of the Indi-ans, which liued like the Alarbes, hauing no setled place,* and fed vpon *Tunas* and rootes of the fields, and wilde beasts that they killed. Which if it were so, if they should enter into it and finde no victuals to passe the winter, they could not chuse but perish. For they were entred alreadie into the beginning of October: and if they staied any longer, they were not able to returne for raine and snowes, nor to sustaine themselues in so poore a countrey. The Gouernour (that desired long to see himselfe in a place where hee might sleepe his full sleep, rather then to conquer and gouerne a coun-trie where so many troubles presented themselues) presently returned back that same way that he came.

No trauelling by land with-out an inter-pretour.

V   Chap.

Chap. XXXV.

How they returned to Nilco, *and came to* Minoya, *where they agreed to make ships to depart out of the land of* Florida.

Hen that which was determined was publiſhed in the Campe, there were many that were greatly grieued at it: for they held the Sea voyage as doubtfull, for the euill meanes they had, and of as great danger, as the trauelling by land: and they hoped to finde ſome rich countrie before they came to the land of the Chriſtians, by that which *Cabeça de Vaca* had told the Emperour: and that was this; That after hee had found clothes made of cotton wooll, hee ſaw gold ànd ſiluer, and ſtones of great value. And they had not yet come where hee had been. For vntill that place hee alwaies trauélled by the Sea coaſt: and they trauelled farre within the land; and that going toward the Weſt, of neceſſitie they ſhould come where hee had been. For he ſaid, That in a certain place he trauelled many daies, and entred into the land toward the North. And in *Guaſco* they had alreadie found ſome Turkie ſtones, and mantles of cotton wooll: which the Indians ſignified by ſignes that they had from the Weſt: and that holding that courſe they ſhould draw neere to the land of the Chriſtians. But though they were much diſcontented with it, and it grieued many to goe backward, which would rather haue aduentured their liues and haue died in the land of *Florida,* then to haue gone

poore

Gold, ſiluer and precious ſtones in Florida.

Turkie ſtones and mantles of cotton wooll found in Guaſco.

ouble almoſt all the Indians that ſerued them died.
nd after they were in *Minoya,* many Chriſtians alſo
ed: and the moſt part were ſicke of great and dange-
us diſeaſes, which had a ſpice of the lethargie. At
place died *Andrew de Vaſconcelos,* and two Portu-
of *Eluas,* which were very neere him: which were
hren, and by their ſurname called *Sotis.* The Chri-
s lodged in one of the townes, which they liked
which was fenſed about, and diſtant a quarter
eague from the Great Riuer. The Maiz that was
other towne was brought thither; and in all it
ſeemed to bee 6000. hanegs or buſhels. And
was the beſt timber to make ſhips, that they had
n all the land of *Florida:* wherefore all of them
od great thankes for ſo ſingular a fauour, and
hat that which they deſired would take effect
was, that they might ſafely bee conducted into
of the Chriſtians.

CHAP. XXXVI.

ere were ſeuen Brigandines builded, and how th
rted from Minoya.

Sſoone as they came to *Minoya,* th
Gouernor commanded them to g
ther all the chaines together, whi
euerie one had to lead Indians i
and to gather al the yron which th
had for their prouiſion, and al the r
e Camp: and to ſet vp a forge to ma
mmanded them to cut downe timber
s. And a Portugall of *Ceuta,* who haui
n *Fez,* had learned to ſaw timber wit

lo

poore out of it: yet were they not a ſufficient part to
hinder that which was determined, becauſe the principall men agreed with the Gouernour. And afterward
there was one that ſaid, hee would put out one of his
owne eyes, to put out another of *Luis de Moſcoſo;* becauſe it would grieue him much to ſee him proſper:
becauſe aſwell himſelf as others of his friends had croſ-
ſed that which hee durſt not haue done, ſeeing that
within two daies hee ſhould leaue the gouernment.
From *Dayeao,* where now they were, to *Rio grande,* or
the Great Riuer, was 150 leagues: which vnto that
place they had gone Weſtward. And by the way as
they returned backe they had much adoe to find Maiz
to eate: for where they had paſſed, the countrey was
deſtroyed: and ſome little Maiz that was left the Indians had hidden. The townes which in *Naguatex*
they had burned (whereof it repented them) were repaired againe, and the houſes full of Maiz. This countrie is well inhabited and plentifull. In that place are
veſſels made of clay, which differ very little from
thoſe of *Eſtremoz,* or *Monte-mor.* In *Chaguate* the Indians by commandement of the Cacique came peaceably, and ſaid, that the Chriſtian which remained there
would not come. The Gouernour wrote vnto him,
and ſent him inke and paper that he might anſwere.
The ſubſtance of the words of the letter was to declare
vnto him his determination, which was, to goe out of
the land of *Florida,* and to put him in remembrance
that he was a Chriſtian, that hee would not remaine in
the ſubiection of Infidels, that hee pardoned him the
fault which he had done in going away to the Indians,
that hee ſhould come vnto him: and if they did ſtay
him, that hee would aduertiſe him thereof by writing.

150 leagues betweene the Riuer of Day-cao, and Rio grande.

Naguatex.

Fine earthen veſſels. Chaguate.

The Indian went with the letter, and came again without any more answere, then, on the back side, his name and his seale, that they might know he was aliue. The Gouernour sent twelue horsemen to seeke him: but he, which had his spies, so hid himselfe, that they could not find him. For want of Maiz the Gouernour could not stay any longer to seeke him. Hee departed from *Chaguete,* and passed the Riuer by *Aays;* going downe by it hee found a towne called *Chilano,* which as yet they had not seen. They came to *Nilco,* & found so little Maiz, as could not suffice till they made their ships; because the Christians, being in *Guachoya* in the seede time, the Indians for feare of them durst not come to sow the grounds of *Nilco:* and they knew not thereabout any other countrie where any Maiz was: and that was the most fruitfull soile that was thereaway, and where they had most hope to finde it. Euery one was confounded, and the most part thought it bad counsell to come backe from the Riuer of *Daycao,* and not to haue followed their fortune, going that way that went ouer land. For by Sea it seemed impossible to saue themselues, vnlesse God would worke a miracle for them: for there was neither Pilot, nor Sea-chart, neither did they know where the Riuer entred into the Sea, neither had they notice of it, neither had they any thing wherewith to make sailes, nor any store of Enequem, which is a grasse whereof they make Okam, which grew there: and that which they found they saued to calke the Pinaces withall, neither had they any thing to pitch them withall: neither could they make ships of such substance, but that any storme would put thé in great danger: and they feared much it would fall out with them, as it did with *Pamphilo de Naruaez,*

Aays.
Chilano.
Nilco.

long saw, which for such purposes they had carried with them, did teach others, which helped him to saw timber. And a *Genowis*, whom it pleased God to preserue (for without him they had neuer come out of the countrie: for there was neuer another that could make ships but hee) with foure or fiue other *Biscaine* carpenters, which hewed his plancks and other timbers, made the brigandines: And two calkers, the one of *Genua*, the other of *Sardinia* did calke them with the tow of an hearb like hempe, whereof before I haue made mention, which there is named Encquen. And because there was not enough of it, they calked them with the flaxe of the Countrie, and with the mantles, which they rauelled for that purpose. A cooper which they had among them fell sicke, and was at the point of death: and there was none other that had any skill in that trade: it pleased God to send him his health: And albeit he was verie weake, and could not labour; yet 15. daies before they departed, he made for euery brigandine two halfe hogs heads, which the mariners call quarterets, because foure of them hold a pipe of water. The Indians which dwelt two daies iournie aboue the Riuer in a Prouince called *Taguanate*, and likewise those of *Nilco* and *Guacoya*, and others their neighbours seeing the brigandines in making, thinking, because their places of refuge are in the water, that they were to goe to seeke them: and because the Gouernour demanded mantles of them, as necessarie for sailes, came many times, and brought many mantles, and great store of fish. And for certaine it seemed that God was willing to fauour them in so great necessitie, moouing the minds of the Indians to bring them: for to goe to take them, they were neuer able. For in the towne

where

Marginal notes:

Enequen is an herbe like Hempe.

Flaxe of the countrie.

Taguanate two daies iourney aboue Minoya.

where they were, assoone as winter came in, they were so inclosed and compassed with water, ỹ they could go no farther by land, then a league, & a league & an half. And if they would go father, they could carrie no horses, & without thẽ they were not able to fight with the Indians, because they were many: and so many for so many on foote they had the aduantage of them by water and by land, because they were more apt and lighter, and by reason of the disposition of the Countrie, which was according to their desire for the vse of their warre. They brought also some cords, and those which wanted for cables were made of the barkes of Mulberrie trees. They made stirrops of wood, & made ankers of their stirrops. In the moneth of March, when it had not rained a moneth before, the Riuer grew so big, that it came to *Nilco*, which was nine leagues off: and on the other side, the Indians said, that it reached other nine leagues into the land. In the towne where the Christians were, which was somewhat high ground, where they could best goe, the water reached to the stirrops. They made certaine rafts of timber, and laid manie boughes vpon them, wheron they set their horses, and in the houses they did the like. But seeing that nothing preuailed, they went vp to the lofts: and if they went out of the houses, it was in canoes, or on horseback in those places where the ground was hiest. So they were two moneths, and could doe nothing, during which time the Riuer decreased not. The Indians ceased not to come vnto the brigantines as they were wont, and came in canoes. At that time the Gouernour feared they would set vpon him. Hee commanded his men to take an Indian secretly of those that came to the towne, and to stay him till the rest were

Side notes:

The great vse of horses.

Mulberrie trees.

The mightie increasing of the Riuer for two moneths space, to wit, all March and Aprill.

were gone : and they tooke one. The Gouernour commanded him to bee put to torture, to make him confesse, whether the Indians did practise any treason or no. Hee confessed that the Caciques of *Nilco, Guachoya,* & *Taguanate,* and others, which in al were about 20. Caciques, with a great number of people, determined to come vpon him; and that three daies before, they would send a great present of fish to colour their great treason and malice, and on the verie day they would send some Indians before with another present: And these with those which were our slaues, which were of their conspiracie also, should set the houses on fire, and first of all possesse themselues of the lances which stood at the doores of the houses; and the Caciques with all their men should bee neere the towne in ambush in the wood, and when they saw the fire kindled, should come, and make an end of the conquest. The Gouernour commanded the Indian to be kept in a chaine, and the selfesame day that he spake of, there came 30. Indians with fish. Hee commanded their right hands to be cut off, and sent them so backe to the Cacique of *Guachoya,* whose men they were. He sent him word, that he and the rest should come when they would, for he desired nothing more, and that hee should know, that they thought not any thing which he knew not before they thought of it. Hereupon they all were put in a very great feare : And the Caciques of *Nilco* and *Taguanate* came to excuse themselues : and a few daies after came he of *Guachoya,* and a principal Indian and his subiect, said, he knew by certaine information, That the Caciques of *Nilco* and *Taguanate* were agreed to come and make warre vpon the Christians. Assoone as ỹ Indians came from *Nilco,* the Gouernour

The grand conspiracie of the Indians against the Christians.

Note well.

Thirtie Indians of the Cacique of Guachoya haue their right hands cut off.

X

uernour examined them, and they confeſſed it was true. Hee deliuered them preſently to the principall man of *Guachoya,* which drew them out of the towne and killed them. Another day came ſome from *Taguanate,* and confeſſed it likewiſe. The Gouernour commanded their right hands and noſes to be cut off, and ſent them to the Cacique, wherewith they of *Guachoya* remained very well contented : and they came oftentimes with preſents of mantles and fiſh, and hogs, which bred in the Countrie of ſome ſwine that were loſt by the way the laſt yeere. Aſſoone as the waters were ſlaked, they perſwaded the Gouernour to ſend men to *Taguanate:* They came and brought canoes, wherein the footemen were conueied downe the Riuer, and a Captaine with horſemen went by land ; and the Indians of *Guachoya,* which guided him, till they came to *Taguanate,* aſſaulted the towne, and took many men and women, and mantles, which with thoſe that they had alreadie were ſufficient to ſupplie their want. The brigandines being finiſhed in the moneth of Iune, the Indians hauing told vs, That the Riuer increaſed but once a yeere, when the ſnowes did melt, in the time wherein I mentioned it had alreadie increaſed, being now in ſommer, and hauing not rained a long time, it pleaſed God, that the flood came vp to the towne to ſeeke the brigandines, from whence they carried them by water to the Riuer. Which, if they had gone by land, had been in danger of breaking and ſplitting their keeles, and to bee all vndone ; becauſe that for want of iron, the ſpikes were ſhort, and the planckes and timber were very weake. The Indians of *Minoya,* during the time that they were there, came to ſerue them (being driuen thereunto by neceſſity)

The right hands and noſes of traitours cut off.

Hogges in Florida.

Taguanate taken.

Iune.
The Riuer increaſeth but once a yeere when the ſnowes doe melt in March and Aprill.
A miraculous acident.

sity)that of the Maiz which they had taken from them,
they would bestow some crummes vpon them. And
because the Countrie was fertill, and the people vsed
to feed of Maiz, and the Christians had gotten all from
them that they had, and the people were many, they
were not able to sustaine themselues. Those which
came to the towne were so weake and feeble, that they
had no flesh left on their bones: and many came and
died neere the towne for pure hunger and weakenesse.
The Gouernour commanded vpon grieuous punish-
ments to giue them no Maiz. Yet, when they saw that
the hogges wanted it not, and that they had yeelded
themselues to serue them, & considering their miserie
and wretchednes, hauing pity of thē, they gaue them
part of the Maiz which they had. And when the time
of their embarkment came, there was not sufficient to
serue their owne turnes. That which there was, they
put into the brigandines, and into great canoes tied
two and two together. They shipped 22. of the best
horses, that were in the Camp, the rest they made dried
flesh of; and dressed the hogges which they had in like
manner. They departed from *Minoya* the second day
of Iulie, 1543.

Chap. XXXVII.

*As the Christians went downe the great Riuer on their
voyage, the Indians of* Quigalta *did set vpon them,
and what was the successe thereof.*

THe day before they departed from *Minoya*,
they determined to dismisse al the men & women of the Countrie, which they had detained as slaues to serue them, saue some hundred, little

more or leſſe,which the Gouernour embarked,and others whom it pleaſed him to permit. And becauſe there were many men of qualitie, whom he could not deny that which he granted to others,he vſed a policy, ſaying, that they might ſerue them as long as they were in the Riuer,but when they came to the ſea, they muſt ſend them away for want of water, becauſe they had but few veſſels. He told his friends in ſecret, that they ſhould carrie theirs to *Nueua Eſpanna :* And all thoſe whom hee bare no good will vnto (which were the greater number) ignorant of that which was hidden from them, which afterward time diſcouered, thinking it inhumanitie for ſo little time of ſeruice, in reward of the great ſeruice that they had done them,to carrie them with them, to leaue them ſlaues to other

500. Slaues left in the Countrie.

men out of their owne Countries ; left fiue hundred men and women;among whom were many boies and girles,which ſpake & vnderſtood the Spaniſh tongue. The moſt of them did nothing but weepe: which mooued great compaſſion ; ſeeing that all of them with good will would haue become Chriſtians, and were left in ſtate of perdition. There went from *Minoya* 322 Spaniards in ſeuen brigandines, well made,

They ſaile downe Rio Grande from Minoya 17. daies before they came to the mouth thereof.

ſaue that the plankes were thin,becauſe the nailes were ſhort,and were not pitched,nor had any decks to keep the water from comming in. In ſtead of decks they laid planks,whereon the mariners might runne to trim their ſailes, and the people might refreſh themſelues aboue and below. The Gouernour made his Captaines,and gaue to euery one his brigandine, and took their oth and their word, that they would obey him, vntill they came to the land of the Chriſtians. The Gouernour tooke one of the brigandines for himſelf,

which

which he best liked. The same day that they departed from *Minoya*, they passed by *Guachoya*, where the Indians tarried for them in canoes by the Riuer. And on the shore, they had made a great arbour with boughes: They desired him to come on shore; but he excused himselfe, and so went along: The Indians in their canoes accompanied him; and comming where an arme of the Riuer declined on the right hand, they said, that the Prouince of *Quigalta* was neere vnto that place, and importuned the Gouernour to set vpon him, and that they would aide him. And because they had said, that he dwelt three daies iournie downe the Riuer, the Gouernour supposed that they had plotted some treason against him, and there left them; and went downe with the greatest force of the water. The current was very strong, and with the helpe of ores, they went very swiftly. The first day they landed in a wood on the left hand of the Riuer, and at night they withdrew themselues to the brigandines. The next day they came to a towne, where they went on shore, and the people that was in it durst not tarrie. A woman that they tooke there being examined, said, that that towne belonged to a Cacique named *Huasene*, subiect to *Quigalta*, and that *Quigalta* tarried for them below in the Riuer with many men. Certaine horsemen went thither, and found some houses, wherein was much Maiz. Immediately more of them went thither and tarried there one day, in which they did beate out, and tooke as much Maiz as they needed. While they were there, many Indians came from the nether part of the Riuer, and on the other side right against them somewhat carelessely set themselues in order to fight. The Gouernour sent in two canoes the crossebowmen

The second day.

Huasene.

Another day.

X 3　　　　*that*

that he had, and as many more as could goe in them.
They ran away, and feeing the Spaniards could not o-
uertake them, they returned backe, and tooke courage;
and comming neerer, making an outcrie, they threatned them : and affoone as they departed thence, they
went after them, fome in canoes, and fome by land a-
long the Riuer; and getting before, comming to a
towne that ftood by the Riuers fide, they ioyned al together, making a fhew that they would tarrie there.
Euerie brigandine towed a canoe faftened to their
fternes for their particular feruice. Prefently there entred men into euerie one of them, which made the Indians to flie, and burned the towne. The fame day
they prefently landed in a great field, where the Indians durft not tarrie. The next day there were gathered
together an hundred canoes, among which were fome
that carried 60. and 70. men, and the principall mens
canoes had their tilts, and plumes of white and red
feathers for their enfignes : and they came within two
croffebow fhot of the brigandines, and fent three Indians in a fmall canoe with a fained meffage to view the
manner of the brigandines, and what weapons they
had. And comming to the fide of the Gouernours
brigandine, one of the Indians entred, and faid :

*A towne bur-
ned.*

The third day.

*A fleete of an
hundred faire
and great ca-
noes.*

That the Cacique of Quigalta *his Lord, fent him his
commendations, and did let him vnderftand, that all that
the Indians of* Guachoya *had told him concerning himfelfe, was falfe, and that they had incenfed him, becaufe they
were his enemies; that he was his feruant, and fhould find
him fo.*

The Gouernour anfwered him, that he beleeued all
that he faid was true, and willed him to tell him, that he
efteemed his friendfhip very much. With this anfwer
they

they returned to the place where the rest in their canoes were waiting for them, and from thence all of them fell downe, and came neere the Spaniards, shouting aloud, and threatning of them. The Gouernour sent *Iohn de Guzman*, which had been a Captaine of footemen in *Florida*, with 15. armed men in canoes to make them giue way. Assoone as the Indians saw them come towards them, they diuided themselues into two parts, and stood still till the Spaniards came nie them, and when they were come neere them, they ioyned together on both sides, taking *Iohn de Guzman* in the middest, and them that came first with him, and with great furie borded them : And as their canoes were bigger, and many of them leaped into the water to stay them, and to lay hold on the canoes of the Spaniards, and ouerwhelme them; so presently they ouerwhelmed them. The Christians fell into the water, and with the weight of their armour sunke downe to the bottome: and some few, that by swimming or holding by the canoe could haue saued themselues, with oares and staues, which they had, they strooke them on the head and made them sinke. When they of the brigandines saw the ouerthrow, though they went about to succour them, yet through the current of the Riuer they could not goe backe. Foure Spaniards fled to the brigandine that was neerest to the canoes; and only these escaped of those that came among the Indians. They were eleuen that died there : among whom *Iohn de Guzman* was one, and a sonne of *Don Carlos*, called *Iohn de Vargas* : the rest also were persons of accout and men of great courage. Those that escaped by swimming, said, that they saw the Indians enter the

Eleuen Spaniards drowned.
The death of Iohn de Guzman.

canoe

canoe of *Iohn de Guzman* at the sterne of one of their canoes, and whether they carried him away dead or aliue they could not certainly tell.

Chap. XXXVIII.
Which declareth how they were pursued by the Indians.

He Indians, seeing that they had gotten the victorie, tooke such courage, that they assaulted them in the brigandines, which they durst not doe before. They came first to that brigandine wherein *Calderon* went for Captaine, and was in the rereward: and at the first volie of arrowes they wounded 25 men. There were only foure armed men in this brigandine: these did stand at the brigandines side to defend it. Those that were vnarmed, seeing how they hurt them, left their oares and went vnder the deck: whereupon the brigandine began to crosse, and to goe where the current of the streame carried it. One of the armed men seeing this, without the commandement of the Captaine, made a footman to take an oare and stirre the brigandine, hee standing before him and defending him with his target. The Indians came no neerer then a bowshot, from whence they offended and were not offended, receiuing no hurt: for in euery brigandine was but one crossebow, and those which wee had were very much out of order. So that the Christians did nothing else but stand for a butte to receiue their arrowes. Hauing left this brigandine they went to another, and fought with

2 5. Spaniards wounded.

The great vse of large targets.

with it halfe an houre; and so from one to another they fought with them all. The Christians had mattes to lay vnder them, which were double, and so close and strong, that no arrow went thorow them. And assoone as the Indians gaue them leisure, they fensed the brigandines with them. And the Indians seeing that they could not shoote leuell, shot their arrowes at randon vp into the aire, which fell into the brigandines, and hurt some of the men : and not therewith contented, they sought to get to them which were in the canoes with the horses. Those of the brigandines enuironed them to defend them, and tooke them among them. Thus seeing themselues much vexed by them, and so wearied that they could no longer endure it, they determined to trauell all the night following, thinking to get beyond the countrie of *Quigalta*, and that they would leaue them : but when they thought least of it, supposing they had now left them, they heard very neere them so great outcries, that they made them deafe, and so they followed vs all that night, and the next day till noone, by which time we were come into the countrie of others, whom they desired to vse vs after the same manner; and so they did. The men of *Quigalta* returned home; and the other in fiftie canoes fought with vs a whole day and a night: and they entred one of the brigandines, that came in the rereward by the canoe which she had at her sterne, and tooke away a woman which they found in it, and afterward hurt some of the men of the brigandines. Those which came with the horses in the canoes, being wearie with rowing night and day, lingered behind; and presently the Indians came vpon them, and they of the brigandines tarried for them. The Gouer-

Strong mats a good defence against arrowes.

Another Prouince.

Y   nour

nour refolued to goe on fhore and to kill the horfes, because of the flow way which they made because of them. Affoone as they faw a place conuenient for it,

Dried horfe-flefh for food. they went thither and killed the horfes, and brought the flefh of them to drie it aboord. Foure or fiue of them remained on fhore aliue : the Indians went vnto them, after the Spaniards were embarked. The horfes were not acquainted with them, and began to neigh, and runne vp and downe, in fuch fort, that the Indians, for feare of them, leaped into the water : and getting into their canoes went after the brigandines, fhooting cruelly at them. They followed vs that euening and the night following till the next day at tenne of the clocke, and then returned vp the Riuer. Prefently from

A fmal towne. a fmall towne that ftood vpon the Riuer came feuen canoes, and followed vs a little way downe the Riuer, fhooting at vs : but feeing they were fo few that they could doe vs but little harme, they returned to their towne. From thence forward, vntill they came to the

They failed 17. daies downe the Riuer, which is about 250. leagues. Sea, they had no encounter. They failed downe the Riuer feuenteene daies : which may be two hundred and fifty leagues iourney, little more or leffe : and neere vnto the Sea the Riuer is diuided into two armes, each of them is a league and an halfe broad.

Chap. XXXIX.

How they came vnto the fea: and what happened vnto them in all their voiage.

Alfe a league before they came to the fea, they came to anker to reft themfelues there about a day : for they were very weary with rowing

and

and out of heart. For by the space of many daies they had eaten nothing but parched and sodden Maiz; which they had by allowance euery day an headpeece ful by strike for euery three mē. While they rode there at anker seuen canoes of Indians came to set vpō those, which they brought with them. The Gouernour commanded armed men to go aboord them, and to driue them farther off. They came also against them by land through a thick wood, and a moorish ground, and had staues with very sharp forked heads made of the bones of fishes, and fought verie valiantly with vs, which went out to encounter them. And the other that came in canoes with their arrowes staied for them that came against them, and at their comming both those that were on land, and those in the canoes wounded some of vs: And seeing vs come neere them, they turned their backs, and like swift horses among footemen gat away from vs; making some returnes, and reuniting themselues together, going not past a bow shot off: for in so retiring they shot, without receiuing any hurt of the Christians. For though they had some bowes, yet they could not vse them; and brake their armes with rowing to ouertake them. And the Indians easily in their compasse went with their canoes, staying and wheeling about as it had been in a skirmish, perceiuing that those that came against them could not offend them. And the more they stroue to come neere them, the more hurt they receiued. Assoone as they had driuen them farther off, they returned to the brigandines. They staied two daies there : And departed from thence vnto the place, where the arme of the Riuer entreth into the sea. They sounded in the Riuer neere vnto the Sea, and found 40. fathoms water. They

staied

staied there. And the Gouernour commanded al and
singular persons to speake their minds touching their
voiage, whether it were best to crosse ouer to *Nueua Espanna*, committing théselues to the hie sea, or whether
they should keepe along the coast. There were sundry
opinions touching this matter : wherein *Iohn Danusco,*
which presumed much, and tooke much vpon him in
the knowledge of nauigation, and matters of the sea,
although hee had but little experience, mooued the
Gouernour with his talke : and his opinion was se-
conded by some others. And they affirmed, that it was
much better to passe by the hie sea, and crosse the
gulfe, which was three of foure parts the lesser trauell,
because in going along ý coast, they went a great way
about, by reason of the compasse, which the land did
make. *Iohn Danusco* said, that he had seene the seacard,
and that from the place where they were, the coast ran
East and West vnto *Rio de las Palmas* ; and from *Rio de
las Palmas* to *Nueua Espanna* from North to South : and
therefore in sailing alwaies in sight of land would bee
a great compassing about and spending of much time ;
& that they would be in great danger to be ouertaken
with winter before they should get to the land of the
Christians : and that in 10. or 12. daies space, hauing
good weather, they might bee there in crossing ouer.
The most part were against this opinion, and said, that
it was more safe to go along the coast, though they staied the longer : because their ships were very weake
and without decks, so that a very little storme was e-
nough to cast them away : and if they should be hin-
dred with calmes, or contrarie weather, through the
small store of vessels which they had to carrie water in,
they should likewise fall into great danger : and that
although

although the ships were such as they might venture in them, yet hauing neither Pilot nor Seacard to guide themselues, it was no good counsell to crosse the gulfe. This opinion was confirmed by the greatest part : and they agreed to go along the coast. At the time wherein they sought to depart from thence, the cable of the anker of the Gouernours brigandine brake, and the anker remained in the Riuer. And albeit, they were neere the shore, yet it was so deepe, that the Diuers diuing many times could neuer find it : which caused great sadnes in the Gouernour, and in all those that went with him in his brigandine : But with a grindstone which they had, and certaine bridles which remained to some of the Gentlemen, and men of worship which had horses, they made a weight which serued in stead of an anker. The 18. of Iuly, they went foorth to sea with faire and prosperous weather for their voiage. And seeing that they were gone two or three leagues from the shore, the Captaines of the other brigandines ouertooke them, and asked the Gouernour, wherefore he did put off from the shore ? and that if he would leaue the coast, he should say so ; and he should not do it without the consent of all : and that if hee did otherwise, they would not follow him, but that euery one would doe what seemed best vnto himselfe. The Gouernour answered, that hee would doe nothing without their counsell, but that hee did beare off from the land to saile the better and safer by night ; and that the next day when time serued, he would returne to the sight of land againe. They sailed with a reasonable good wind that day and the night following, and the next day till euening song, alwaies in fresh water : whereat they wondred much : for they were verie

They landed the 30. of May, 1539. Chap. 7. they went foorth to sea Iuly 18. 1543.

Fresh water almost two daies sailing in the Sea.

Y 3

very farre from land. But the force of the current of
the Riuer is ſo great, and the coaſt there is ſo ſhallow
and gentle, that the freſh water entreth farre into the
Sea. That euening on their right hand they ſaw certaine creekes, whither they went, and reſted there that
night : where *Iohn Danuſco* with his reaſons wonne
them at laſt, that all conſented and agreed to commit
themſelues to the maine Sea, alleaging, as he had done
before, that it was a great aduantage, and that their
voyage would be much ſhorter. They ſailed two daies,
and when they would haue come to ſight of land they
could not, for the winde blew from the ſhore. On the
fourth day, ſeeing their freſh water began to faile, fearing neceſſitie and danger, they all complained of *Iohn*
Danuſco, and of the Gouernour that followed his coun-
ſell : and euery one of the Captaines ſaid, that they
would no more goe from the ſhore, though the Gouernour went whither he would. It pleaſed God that
the winde changed though but a little : and at the end
of foure daies after they had put to ſea, being alreadie
deſtitute of water, by force of rowing they got within
ſight of land, and with great trouble recouered it, in an
open roade. That euening the winde came to the
South, which on that coaſt is a croſſe winde, and draue
the brigandines againſt the ſhore, becauſe it blew very
hard, and the anchors were ſo weake, that they yeelded
and began to bend. The Gouernour commanded all
men to leape into the water, and going between them
and the ſhore, and thruſting the brigandines into the
Sea aſſoone as the waue was paſt, they ſaued them till
the winde ceaſed.

The coaſt
ſhallow.

Certaine
creekes where
they reſted a
night.

An open
Roade.

CHAP.

Chap. XL.

How they lost one another by a storme, and afterward came together in a creeke.

IN the bay where they rode, after the tempest was past, they went on shore, and with mattockes, which they had, they digged certaine pits, which grew full of fresh water, where they filled all the cask which they had. The next day they departed thence, and sailed two daies, and entred into a creeke like vnto a poole, fenced from the South winde, which then did blow, and was against them : and there they staied foure daies, not being able to get out : and when the Sea was calme they rowed out : they sailed that day, and toward euening the winde grew so strong that it draue them on the shore, and they were sorie that they had put foorth from the former harbour : for as soone as night approched a storme began to rise in the Sea, and the winde still waxed more and more violent with a tempest. The brigandines lost one another : two of them, which bare more into the Sea, entred into an arme of the Sea, which pearced into the land two leagues beyond the place where the other were that night. The fiue which staied behinde, being alwaies a league, and halfe a league the one from the other, met together, without any knowledge the one of the other, in a wilde roade, where the winde and the waues droue them on shore : for their anchors did streighten and came home; and they could not rule their oares, putting seuen or eight men to euery oare, which rowed to seaward : and all the rest leaped into

Fresh water is commonlie found by digging in the sands on the sea side.

An arme of the sea.

A wild roade.

the

the water, and when the waue was past that draue the brigandine on shore, they thrust it againe into Sea with all the diligence and might that they had. Others, while another waue was in comming, with bowles laued out the water that came in ouerboord. While they were in this tempest in great feare of being cast away in that place, from midnight forward they endured an

A swarme of grieuous Moskitoes.

intollerable tormēt of an infinite swarme of Moskitoes which fell vpon them, which assoone as they had stung the flesh, it so infected it, as though they had bin venomous. In the morning the Sea was asswaged and the wind slaked, but not the Muskitoes : for ȳ sailes which were white seemed blacke with them in the morning. Those which rowed, vnlesse others kept them away, were not able to row. Hauing passed the feare & danger of the storme, beholding the deformities of their faces, and the blowes which they gaue themselues to driue them away, one of them laughed at another. They met all together in the creek where the two brigandines were, which outwent their fellowes. There

A skumme of the sea like pitch, called Copee.

was found a skumme, which they call Copee, which the Sea casteth vp, and it is like pitch, wherewith in some places, where pitch is wanting, they pitch their ships : there they pitched their brigandines. They rested two daies, and then eftsoones proceeded on their voyage. They sailed two daies more, and landed in a

Another deep bay.

Bay or arme of the Sea, where they staied two daies. The same day that they went from thence sixe men went vp in a canoe toward the head of it, and could not see the end of it. They put out from thence with a South winde, which was against them : but because it was little, and for the great desire they had to shorten their voyage, they put out to sea by force of oares, and

for

for all that made very little way with great labour in two daies, and went vnder the lee of a small Island into an arme of the Sea, which compassed it about. While they were there, there fell out such weather, that they gaue God many thankes, that they had found out such an harbour. There was great store of fish in that place, which they tooke with nets, which they had, and hookes. Heere a man cast an hooke and a line into the Sea, and tied the end of it to his arme, and a fish caught it, and drew him into the water vnto the necke: and it pleased God that hee remembred himselfe of a knife that he had, and cut the line with it. There they abode fourteene daies: and at the end of them it pleased God to send them faire weather, for which with great deuotion they appointed a procession, and went in procession along the strand, beseeching God to bring them to a land, where they might serue him in better sort.

A small Island.

Great store of fish.

Fourteene daies abode in this place.

Chap. XLI.
How they came to the Riuer of Panuco in Nueua Espanna.

I N all the coast wheresoeuer they digged they found fresh water: there they filled their vessels; and the procession being ended, embarked themselues, and going alwaies in sight of the shore they sailed sixe daies. *Iohn Danusco* said that it would doe well to beare out to seaward: for he had seene the Sea-card, and remembred that from *Rio de las Palmas* forward the coast did runne from North to South, and thitherto they had runne from East to West, and in his opinion, by his reckoning, *Rio de las Palmas* could not

Sixe daies sailing.

Z   be

be farre off, from where they were. That same night
they put to sea, and in the morning they saw Palme

leaues floting, and the coast, which ranne North and
South : from midday forward they saw great Mountaines, which vntill then they had not seene : for from

this place to *Puerto de Spiritu Santo*, where they first
landed in *Florida*, was a very plaine and low countrey:
and therfore it cannot be descried, vnlesse a man come
very neere it. By that which they saw, they thought
that they had ouershot *Rio de Palmas* that night,
which is 60 leagues from the Riuer of *Panuco*, which
is in *Nueua Espanna*. They assembled all together,
and some said it was not good to saile by night, lest they
should ouershoot the Riuer of *Panuco*: and others said,
it was not well to lose time while it was fauourable,
and that it could not be so neere that they should passe
it that night : and they agreed to take away halfe the
sailes, and so saile all night. Two of the brigandines,
which sailed that night with all their sailes, by breake
of day had ouershot the Riuer of *Panuco* without seeing it. Of the fiue that came behind, the first that came
vnto it was that wherein *Calderan* was Captaine. A
quarter of a league before they came at it, and before
they did see it, they saw the water muddie, and knew
it to be fresh water: and comming right against the Riuer, they saw, where it entred into the Sea, that the water brake vpon a shold. And because there was no man
there that knew it, they were in doubt whether they
should goe in, or goe along, and they resolued to goe
in : and before they came vnto the current, they went
close to the shore, and entred into the port: and assoone
as they were come in, they saw Indian men and women apparelled like Spaniards : whom they asked in
what

what countrey they were? They answered in Spanish, that it was the Riuer of *Panuco*, and that the towne of the Christians was 15 leagues vp within the land. The ioy that all of them receiued vpon these newes cannot sufficiently be expressed: for it seemed vnto them, that at that instant they were borne again. And many went on shore and kissed the ground, and kneeling on their knees, with lifting vp their hands and eyes to heauen, they all ceased not to giue God thankes. Those which came after, assoone as they saw *Calderan* come to an anchor with his brigandine in the Riuer, presently went thither, and came into the hauen. The other two brigandines which had ouershot the place, put to sea to returne backe to seeke the rest, and could not doe it, because the winde was contrarie and the Sea growne: they were afraid of being cast away, and recouering the shore, they cast anchor. While they rode there a storme arose: and seeing that they could not abide there, much lesse endure at Sea, they resolued to runne on shore; and as the brigandines were but small, so did they draw but little water; and where they were it was a sandie coast. By which occasion the force of their sailes draue them on shore, without any hurt of them that were in them. As those that were in the port of *Panuco* at this time were in great ioy; so these felt a double griefe in their hearts: for they knew not what was become of their fellowes, nor in what countrey they were, and feared it was a countrey of Indian enemies. They landed two leagues below the port: and when they saw themselues out of the danger of the Sea, euery one tooke of that which he had, as much as he could carrie on his backe: and they trauelled vp into the countrey, and found Indians, which told them

The Riuer of Panuco: the towne 15. leagues from the mouth of the Riuer.

Z 2 where

where their fellowes were; and gaue them good entertainement : wherewith their sadnes was turned into ioy, and they thanked God most humbly for their deliuerance out of so many dangers.

Chap. XLII.

How they came to Panuco, *and how they were receiued of the inhabitants.*

They arriued in the Riuer of Panuco, 1543. Septem. 10.

Rom the time that they put out of *Rio Grande* to the sea, at their departure from *Florida*, vntill they arriued in the Riuer of *Panuco* were 52. daies. They came into the Riuer of *Panuco* the 10. of September, 1543. They went vp the Riuer with their brigandines. They trauelled foure daies; and because the wind was but little, and many times it serued them not, because of the many turnings which the Riuer maketh, and the great current, drawing them vp by towing, and that in many places; for this cause they made very little way, and with great labour: and seeing the execution of their desire to be deferred, which was to come among Christians, and to see the celebration of diuine seruice; which so long time they had not seene; they left the brigandines with the mariners, and went by land to *Panuco*. All of them were apparrelled in Deeres skins tanned and died blacke, to wit, cotes, hose, and shooes. When they came to *Panuco*, presently they went to the Church to pray and giue God thankes, that so miraculously had saued them. The townesmen which before were aduertised by the Indians, and knew of their arriual, caried some of them to their houses, and entertained them, whom they knew, and had acquaintance of,

of, or becauſe they were their Countrimen. The Alcalde Mayor tooke the Gouernour home to his houſe:
and commanded al the reſt, aſſoone as they came, to be
lodged 6. & 6. and 10. & 10. according to the habilitie
of euery towneſman. And all of them were prouided
for by their hoſtes of many hennes and bread of Maiz,
and fruites of the Countrie, which are ſuch as be in the
Iſle of *Cuba*, whereof before I haue ſpoken. The towne
of *Panuco* may containe aboue 70. families; the moſt
of their houſes are of lime and ſtone, and ſome made
of timber, and all of them are thatched. It is a poore
Countrie, and there is neither gold nor ſiluer in it: The
inhabitants liue there in great abundance of victuals
and ſeruants. The richeſt haue not aboue 500. crownes
rent a yeere, and that is in cotten clothes, hennes, and
Maiz, which the Indians their ſeruants doe giue them
for tribute. There arriued there of thoſe that came out
of *Florida*, three hundred and eleuen Chriſtians. Preſently the Alcalde Mayor ſent one of the townſmen in
poſt to aduertiſe the Viceroy, *Don Antonio de Mendo-
ça*, which was reſident in *Mexico*, that of ỹ people that
went with *Don Ferdinando de Soto* to diſcouer and conquer *Florida*, three hundred and eleuen men were ariued there, that ſeeing they were imploied in his Male-
ſties ſeruice, he would take ſome order to prouide for
them. Whereat the Viceroy, and all the inhabitants
of *Mexico* wondred. For they thought they were miſ-
carried, becauſe they had trauelled ſo farre within the
maine land of *Florida*, and had no newes of them for
ſo long a time: and it ſeemed a wonderfull thing vnto them, how they could ſaue themſelues ſo long a-
mong Inſidels, without any fort, wherein they might
fortifie themſelues, and without any other ſuccour at

*The deſcrip-
tion of Pa-
nuco.*

*311. Chriſtians
arriued at Pa-
nuco.*

Z 3   all.

all. Presently the Viceroy sent a warrant, wherein hee commãded, that whithersoeuer they sent, they should giue them victuals, and as many Indians for their cariages as they needed : and where they would not furnish them, they might take those things that were necessarie perforce without incurring any danger of law. This warrant was so readilie obeyed, that by the way before they came to the townes, they came to receiue them with hennes, and victuals.

Of the fauour which they found at the hands of the Viceroy, and of the inhabitants of the Citie of Mexico.

Rom *Panuco* to the great Citie *Temistitan Mexico* is 60. leagues ; and other 60. from *Panuco* to the Port *de Vera Cruz*, where they take shipping for *Spaine*, and those that come from *Spaine* do land to go for *Nueua Espanna*. These three townes stand in a triangle : to wit, *Vera Cruz*, to the South, *Panuco* to the North, and *Mexico* to the West, 60. leagues asunder. The Countrie is so inhabited with Indians, that from towne to towne, those which are farthest, are but a league, and halfe a league asunder. Some of them that came from *Florida* staied a moneth in *Panuco* to rest themselues, others fifteene daies, and euery one as long as he listed : for there was none that shewed a sower countenance to his guests, but rather gaue them any thing that they had, and seemed to be grieued when they took their leaue. Which was to be beleeued. For the victuals, which the Indians doe pay them for tribute, are more then they can spend : and in that towne is no commerce ; and there

dwelt

dwelt but few Spaniards there, and they were glad of
their companie. The Alcalde Mayor diuided all
the Emperours clothes which he had (which there
they pay him for his tribute) among thofe that would
come to receiue them. Thofe which had fhirts of maile
left, were glad men : for they had a horfe for one fhirt
of maile : Some horfed themfelues: and fuch as could
not (which were the greateft part) tooke their iournie
on foote : in which they were well receiued of the Indians that were in the townes, and better ferued, then
they could haue been in their owne houfes, though
they had been well to liue. For if they asked one hen
of an Indian, they brought them foure : and if they asked any of the Countrie fruit, though it were a league
off, they ran prefently for it. And if any Chriftian
found himfelf euill at eafe, they carried him in a chaire *This is the*
from one towne to another. In whatfoeuer towne *manner of*
they came, the Cacique, by an Indian which carri- *China, to car-*
ed a rod of Iuftice in his hand, whom they call Ta- *rie men in*
pile, that is to fay, a fergeant, commanded them to *chaires.*
prouide victuals for them, and Indians to beare burdens of fuch things as they had, and fuch as were
needfull to carrie them that were ficke. The Viceroy fent a Portugall 20. leagues from *Mexico*, with
great ftore of fugar, raifons of the Sunne, and con-
ferues, and other things fit for ficke folkes, for fuch as
had neede of them: and had giuen order to cloth them
all at the Emperours charges. And their approch being
knowne by the citizens of *Mexico*, they went out of
the towne to receiue them : and with great courtefie,
requefting them in fauour to come to their houfes, e-
uery one carried fuch as hee met home with him, and
clothed

clothed them euery one the best they could: so that he which had the meanest apparrell, it cost aboue 30. ducats. As many as were willing to come to the Viceroyes house he commanded to be apparelled, and such as were persons of qualitie sate at his table: and there was a table in his house for as many of the meaner sort as would come to it: and he was presently informed, who euery one was, to shew him the courtesie that he deserued. Some of the Cóquerors did set both gentlemen and clownes at their owne table, and many times made the seruant sit cheeke by cheeke by his master: and chiefly the officers and men of base condition did so: for those which had better education did enquire who euery one was, and made difference of persons: but all did what they could with a good will: and euery one told them whom they had in their houses, that they should not trouble themselues, nor thinke themselues the worse, to take that which they gaue them: for they had bin in the like case, and had bin relieued of others, and that this was the custome of that countrey. God reward them all: and God grant, that those which it pleased him to deliuer out of *Florida,* and to bring againe into Christendome, may serue him: and vnto those that died in that countrey, and vnto all that beleeue in him and confesse his holy faith, God for his mercie sake grant the kingdome of heauen. Amen.

CHAP.

Chap. XLIV.

Which declareth some diuersities and particularities of the land of Florida : and the fruites, and beasts, and fowles that are in that Countrie.

Rom the Port *de Spiritu Santo*, where they landed when they entred into *Florida*, to the Prouince of *Ocute*, which may bee 400. leagues, little more or lesse, is a verie plaine Countrie, and hath many lakes and thicke woods, and in some places they are of wild pinetrees; and is a weake soile : There is in it neither Mountaine nor hill. The Countrie of *Ocute* is more fat and fruitfull; it hath thinner woods, and very goodly medows vpon the Riuers. Frō *Ocute* to *Cutifachiqui* may be 130. leagues : 80. leagues thereof are desert, and haue many groues of wild Pine trees. Through the wildernesse great Riuers doe passe. From *Cutifachiqui* to *Xuala*, may be 250. leagues: it is al an hilly Countrie. *Cutifachiqui* and *Xuala* stand both in plaine ground, hie, and haue goodly medows on the Riuers. From thence forward to *Chiaha*, *Coça*, and *Talise*, is plaine ground, dry and fat, and very plentifull of Maiz. From *Xuala* to *Tascaluça* may be 250. leagues. From *Tascaluça* to *Rio Grande*, or ỹ Great Riuer, may be 300. leagues : the Countrie is low, and full of lakes. From *Rio Grande* forward, the Countrie is hier and more champion, and best peopled of all the land of *Florida*. And along this Riuer from *Aquixo* to *Pacaha*, and *Coligoa*, are 150. leagues : the Countrie is plaine, and the woods thinne, and in some places champion, very fruitfull and pleasant. From *Coligoa* to *Autiamque* are

Aa   250.

Marginal notes:

Port de Spiritu Santo is in 29. degrees ½ on the West side of Florida.

Ocute.

Cutifachiqui.

Xuala.

Chiaha, Coça, and Talise.

Tascaluça.

Rio Grande.

Aquixo.

Coligoa.

Autiamque.   250. leagues of hillie Countrie. From *Autiamque* to
Aguacay.   *Aguacay*, may be 230. leagues of plaine ground. From
Aguacay to the Riuer of *Daycao* 120. leagues, all hillie
Countrie.

From the Port *de Spiritu Santo* vnto *Apalache*, they
Pagina 72.   trauelled from East to West, and Northwest. From
Cutifachiqui to *Xuala* from South to North. From
Xuala to *Coça* from East to West. From *Coça* to *Tafca-*
luça, and to *Rio Grande*, as far as the Prouinces of *Quiz-*
quiz and *Aquixo* from East to West. From *Aquixo* to
Pacaha to the North. From *Pacaha* to *Tulla* from East
to West: and from *Tulla* to *Autiamque* from North to
South, to the Prouince of *Guachoya* and *Daycao*.

The bread which they eate in all the land of *Florida*
Maiz.   is of Maiz, which is like courfe millet. And this Maiz
is common in all the Iflandes and West Indies from
the Antiles forward. There are alfo in *Florida* great
Walnuts,   store of Walnuts, and Plummes, Mulberries, and
Plummes,   Grapes. They fow and gather their Maiz euery one
Mulberries,
Grapes.   their feuerall crop. The fruits are common to all : for
they grow abroad in the open fields in great abun-
dance, without any neede of planting or dreffing.
Cheftnuts.   Where there be Mountaines, there be cheftnuts : they
are fomewhat fmaller then the cheftnuts of *Spaine*. Frō
Rio Grande Westward, the Walnuts differ from thofe
soft Walnuts   that grow more Eastward : for they are foft, and like
Eaftward from   vnto Acornes : And thofe which grow from *Rio Gran-*
Rio Grande.
Hard Walnuts   *de* to *Puerto del Spiritu Santo* for the most part are hard ;
Weftward   and the trees and Walnuts in fhew like thofe of *Spaine*.
from Rio
Grande.   There is a fruit through all the Countrie which grow-
eth on a plant like Ligoacan, which the Indians doe
A Peare riall.   plant. The fruit is like vnto Peares Riall : it hath a ve-
rie good fmell, and an excellent tafte. There groweth
another

another plant in the open field, which beareth a fruit like vnto strawberries, close to the ground, which hath a verie good taste. The Plummes are of two kindes, red and gray, of the making and bignesse of nuts, and haue three or foure stones in them. These are better then all the plummes of *Spaine*, and they make farre better Prunes of them. In the Grapes there is onelie want of dressing : for though they bee big, they haue a great kirnell. All other fruits are very perfect, and lesse hurtfull then those of *Spaine*. *Strawberries. Plummes of two kinds.*

There are in *Florida* many Beares, and Lyons, Wolues, Deere, Dogges, Cattes, Marterns and Conies. *Beasts.*

There be many wild Hennes as big as Turkies, Partridges small like those of *Africa*, Cranes, Duckes, Pigeons, Thrushes, and Sparrowes. There are certaine Blacke birds bigger then Sparrows, and lesser then Stares. There are Gosse Hawkes, Falcons, Ierfalcons, and all Fowles of prey that are in *Spaine*. *Fowles.*

The Indians are well proportioned. Those of the plaine Countries are taller of bodie, and better shapen, then those of the Mountaines. Those of the Inland haue greater store of Maiz, and commodities of the Countrie, then those that dwell vpon the sea coast. The Countrie along the sea coast is barren and poore: and the people more warlike. The coast runneth from *Puerto del Spiritu Santo* to *Apalache*, East and West; and from *Apalache* to *Rio de las Palmas* from East to West : from *Rio de las Palmas* vnto *Nueua Espanna* from North to South. It is a gentle coast, but it hath many sholdes, and great shelues of sand.

Deo gratias.

This

This Relation of the discouerie of *Florida* was printed in the house of *Andrew de Burgos*, Printer and Gentleman of the house of my Lord Cardinall the In-
fante.

It was finished the tenth of Februarie in the
yeere one thousand, fiue hundred, fiftie
and seuen, in the noble and most
loyall citie of
Euora.

FINIS.